SARA L. WESTON

Authentic Love: A Guide to creating healthy lesbian relationships

8 Chapter roadmap to finding your authentic self and partner

First edition

This book was professionally typeset on Reedsy.
Find out more at reedsy.com

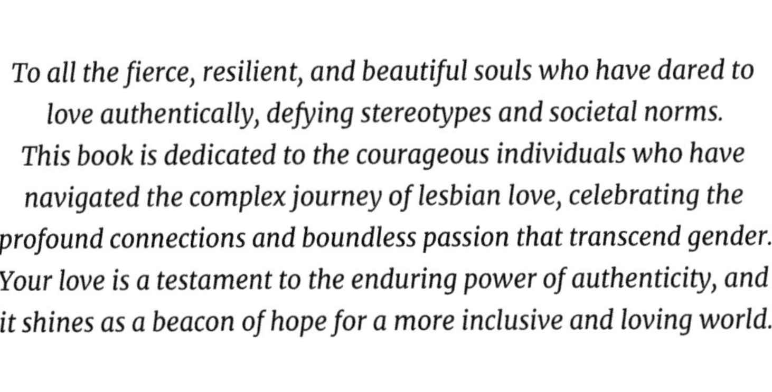

To all the fierce, resilient, and beautiful souls who have dared to love authentically, defying stereotypes and societal norms. This book is dedicated to the courageous individuals who have navigated the complex journey of lesbian love, celebrating the profound connections and boundless passion that transcend gender. Your love is a testament to the enduring power of authenticity, and it shines as a beacon of hope for a more inclusive and loving world.

"In the vast tapestry of love, there are no boundaries, no confines, no limits. Authentic lesbian love is a celebration of the heart's truest desires, a testament to the strength of love in its purest form. It defies expectations, challenges prejudices, and reminds us that love is, and will always be, a force of immeasurable beauty." 🌈❤📚

Contents

Foreword

This eight chapter book offers a comprehensive guide for lesbian women seeking meaningful connections and lasting love. This book goes beyond traditional dating advice and explores the importance of self-awareness, communication, and personal growth in the dating process. Readers will gain valuable tools to navigate the complexities of lesbian dating and create fulfilling relationships based on authenticity and mutual understanding.

This book delves into the unique challenges and joys of lesbian dating. From understanding one's own desires and boundaries to navigating online dating platforms and meeting potential partners, this book provides a step-by-step roadmap for finding the right match. It also addresses common obstacles such as coming out, dealing with rejection, and maintaining healthy relationships. By emphasizing self-love, self-acceptance, and conscious decision-making, readers will learn how to attract and build deep connections with compatible partners.

Readers will develop the skills necessary for building strong and loving relationships. Whether you are new to the dating scene or have been searching for love for a while, this book will empower you to approach dating with intention, authenticity, and a deep understanding of yourself and your desires.

Preface

I wrote this book for all the women who have loved, who've been hurt, who were left with confusion, doubt and felt helpless about ever being able to find a lasting, healthy loving relationship. I've been there too.

1

Chapter 1

Understanding Yourself

1.1 Exploring Your Identity

Understanding and exploring your identity is an essential first step in conscious lesbian dating and love. Your identity encompasses various aspects of who you are, including your sexual orientation, gender identity, values, beliefs, and personal experiences. Taking the time to explore and understand your identity will not only help you gain clarity about yourself but also enable you to navigate the dating world with confidence and authenticity.

Embracing Your Sexual Orientation

As a lesbian, your sexual orientation is a fundamental part of your identity. Embracing and accepting your sexual orientation is crucial for your overall well-being and happiness. It is essential to recognize that being a lesbian is natural, valid, and beautiful. Take pride in who you are and celebrate your unique experiences and perspectives.

Exploring your sexual orientation can be a journey of self-discovery. It may involve reflecting on your past experiences, questioning societal norms, and understanding the different aspects of your attraction to women. Give yourself permission to explore and embrace your desires and attractions without judgment or shame.

Understanding Gender Identity

Gender identity is another important aspect of your identity to explore. While sexual orientation refers to who you are attracted to, gender identity refers to how you identify and experience your own gender. It is essential to recognize that gender identity is diverse and can vary from person to person.

For some lesbians, their gender identity may align with their assigned sex at birth (cisgender). For others, their gender identity may differ from their assigned sex (transgender). It is crucial to respect and validate each individual's gender identity, including your own.

Take the time to reflect on your own gender identity and how it intersects with your sexual orientation. Consider how your gender identity influences your experiences, relationships, and self-perception. Remember that exploring your gender identity is a personal journey, and it is okay to seek support and guidance from trusted friends, mentors, or professionals if needed.

Uncovering Your Values and Beliefs

Understanding your values and beliefs is essential for conscious lesbian dating and love. Your values are the guiding principles that shape your decisions, actions, and relationships. They reflect what is most important to you and what you stand for.

Take some time to reflect on your values and what you prioritize in life. Consider your beliefs about love, relationships, communication, and personal growth. Understanding your values will help you align with partners who share similar beliefs and create a strong foundation for a healthy and fulfilling relationship.

Reflecting on Personal Experiences

Your personal experiences play a significant role in shaping your identity and understanding of yourself. Reflecting on your past relationships, friendships, and life experiences can provide valuable insights into your desires, needs, and patterns.

Consider the lessons you have learned from past relationships and how they have influenced your approach to dating and love. Reflect on the qualities you appreciate in others and the ones that are important to you in a partner. Understanding your past experiences will help you make conscious choices and avoid repeating unhealthy patterns.

Seeking Support and Self-Reflection

Exploring your identity is an ongoing process that requires self-reflection and self-compassion. It is normal to have questions, doubts, and uncertainties along the way. Seeking support from trusted friends, mentors, or therapists can provide valuable guidance and perspective.

Engage in self-reflection practices such as journaling, meditation, or therapy to deepen your understanding of yourself. Take the time to listen to your inner voice, honor your needs, and embrace your authentic self. Remember that self-discovery is a lifelong journey, and each step you take towards understanding your identity brings you closer to finding love and fulfillment.

In the next section, we will delve deeper into understanding your needs and desires, which will further empower you in your journey of conscious lesbian dating and love.

1.2 Understanding Your Needs and Desires

Understanding your needs and desires is a crucial step in conscious lesbian dating. It involves taking the time to reflect on what you truly want and require in a partner and a relationship. By gaining clarity about your needs and desires, you can make informed decisions and attract compatible partners who align with your values and goals. In this section, we will explore various aspects of understanding your needs and desires in the context of lesbian dating.

1.2.1 Reflecting on Your Values and Priorities

To understand your needs and desires, it is essential to reflect on your values and priorities. What are the core principles that guide your life? What qualities and characteristics do you value in a partner? Take some time to think about what matters most to you in a relationship. Consider aspects such as communication, trust, honesty, emotional intimacy, shared interests, and long-term goals. By identifying your values and priorities, you can establish a solid foundation for your dating journey.

1.2.2 Identifying Emotional and Physical Needs

Emotional and physical needs play a significant role in any relationship. It is crucial to identify and understand your emotional and physical needs to ensure a fulfilling and satisfying connection with your partner. Reflect on what makes you feel loved, supported, and emotionally fulfilled. Consider your need for affection, quality time, emotional support, and intimacy. Additionally, think about your physical needs and desires, such as sexual compatibility and attraction. Being aware of these needs will help you communicate them effectively to potential partners.

1.2.3 Exploring Relationship Goals

Understanding your relationship goals is essential in conscious lesbian dating. Take the time to explore what you envision for your future partnership. Are you seeking a long-term committed relationship, or are you open to casual dating? Reflect on your desires for companionship, partnership, and potential family-building. By clarifying your relationship goals, you can attract partners who share similar aspirations and avoid wasting time on incompatible connections.

1.2.4 Assessing Deal Breakers and Boundaries

In conscious lesbian dating, it is crucial to identify your deal breakers and establish healthy boundaries. Deal breakers are non-negotiable aspects that you cannot compromise on in a relationship. These could include values, lifestyle choices, or behaviors that are incompatible with your own. By being aware of your deal breakers, you can avoid getting involved in relationships that are not aligned with your needs and desires. Additionally, setting boundaries is essential for maintaining your emotional well-being and ensuring mutual respect in a relationship. Reflect on your personal boundaries and communicate them clearly to potential partners.

1.2.5 Understanding Love Languages

Love languages refer to the different ways individuals give and receive love. Understanding your love language can help you communicate your needs and desires effectively to your partner. The five love languages are words of affirmation, acts of service, receiving gifts, quality time, and physical touch. Reflect on how you prefer to give and receive love, and consider how your partner's love language aligns with yours. By understanding your love language and that of your partner, you can create a more fulfilling and harmonious relationship.

1.2.6 Embracing Self-Discovery and Growth

Understanding your needs and desires is an ongoing process that requires self-discovery and growth. Take the time to explore yourself, your passions, and your personal growth journey. Engage in activities that bring you joy and help you connect with your authentic self. By continuously learning and growing, you will gain a deeper understanding of your needs and desires, allowing you to attract partners who appreciate and support your personal growth.

1.2.7 Seeking Support and Guidance

Exploring your needs and desires can sometimes be challenging, and seeking support and guidance can be immensely helpful. Consider reaching out to trusted friends, mentors, or therapists who can provide valuable insights and perspectives. Engaging in LGBTQ+ support groups or seeking professional coaching can also offer guidance and support in understanding your needs and desires. Remember, you don't have to navigate this journey alone, and seeking support is a sign of strength.

Understanding your needs and desires is a vital step in conscious lesbian dating. By reflecting on your values, identifying your emotional and physical needs, exploring relationship goals, assessing deal breakers and boundaries, understanding love languages, embracing self-discovery and growth, and seeking support and guidance, you can gain clarity and attract partners who are compatible with your authentic self. Remember, the journey of understanding your needs and desires is ongoing, and it is essential to regularly reassess and communicate them as you grow and evolve.

1.3 Embracing Self-Love and Self-Acceptance

Embracing self-love and self-acceptance is a crucial step in the journey of conscious lesbian dating and love. Before you can truly connect with someone else, it is essential to develop a deep sense of love and acceptance for yourself. This section will explore the importance of self-love, provide practical tips for cultivating it, and discuss the impact it can have on your dating and relationship experiences.

The Power of Self-Love

Self-love is the foundation upon which healthy relationships are built. When you love and accept yourself, you bring a sense of wholeness and authenticity to your interactions with others. It allows you to set healthy boundaries, communicate your needs and desires effectively, and make choices that align with your values and goals.

Embracing self-love also helps you develop a strong sense of self-worth. It enables you to recognize your own value and believe that you deserve love and happiness. This belief is essential in attracting and maintaining healthy relationships. When you love yourself, you become a magnet for partners who appreciate and value you for who you are.

Cultivating Self-Love

Cultivating self-love is an ongoing process that requires self-reflection, self-care, and self-compassion. Here are some practical tips to help you embrace self-love:

1. Practice self-care: Prioritize activities that nourish your mind, body, and soul. This can include engaging in hobbies you enjoy, taking care of your physical health, practicing mindfulness or meditation, and surrounding yourself with positive influences.
2. Challenge negative self-talk: Become aware of the negative thoughts and beliefs you hold about yourself. Replace them with positive affirmations and focus on your strengths and accomplishments. Remember, you are deserving of love and acceptance just as you are.
3. Set healthy boundaries: Learn to say no when something doesn't align with your values or needs. Respect your own boundaries and communicate them clearly to others. This will help you maintain a sense of self-respect and protect your emotional well-being.
4. Practice self-compassion: Treat yourself with kindness and understanding, especially during challenging times. Acknowledge that everyone makes mistakes and that you are worthy of forgiveness and growth. Be gentle with yourself and practice self-compassion when facing setbacks or disappointments.
5. Surround yourself with positive influences: Surround yourself with people who uplift and support you. Seek out friends, mentors, or support groups that align with your values and provide a safe space for personal growth and self-expression.

The Impact on Dating and Relationships

Embracing self-love and self-acceptance has a profound impact on your dating and relationship experiences. When you love and accept yourself, you attract partners who appreciate and value you for who you are. You become less likely to settle for relationships that do not meet your needs or align with your values.

Self-love also empowers you to communicate your needs and desires effectively. You become more assertive in expressing your boundaries and expectations, which fosters healthier and more fulfilling connections. By embracing self-love, you create a strong foundation for building a lasting and meaningful partnership.

Furthermore, self-love allows you to navigate the challenges that may arise in relationships with greater resilience. When you have a strong sense of self-worth, you are less likely to internalize criticism or blame yourself for relationship difficulties. Instead, you can approach conflicts with empathy, understanding, and a willingness to work through them together.

Conclusion

Embracing self-love and self-acceptance is a transformative journey that positively impacts all areas of your life, including your dating and relationship experiences. By cultivating self-love, you develop a strong sense of self-worth, set healthy boundaries, and attract partners who appreciate and value you. Remember, you are deserving of love and happiness, and by embracing self-love, you create the

1.4 Building Confidence and Assertiveness

Building confidence and assertiveness are essential skills for successful dating and finding the right partner. When you feel confident and assertive, you are more likely to attract the right people into your life and create healthy and fulfilling relationships. In this section, we will explore strategies and techniques to help you build confidence and assertiveness in your dating journey.

Embracing Self-Awareness

Before we dive into building confidence and assertiveness, it's important to start with self-awareness. Understanding yourself, your strengths, and your areas for growth is the foundation for building confidence. Take the time to reflect on your values, passions, and goals. What makes you unique? What are your strengths and talents? By embracing self-awareness, you can begin to appreciate and celebrate who you are, which will naturally boost your confidence.

Challenging Limiting Beliefs

Building confidence requires challenging and overcoming limiting beliefs that may hold you back. These beliefs can stem from past experiences, societal expectations, or negative self-talk. Identify any negative beliefs you may have about yourself or dating, such as "I'm not attractive enough" or "I'm not worthy of love." Once you identify these beliefs, challenge them by replacing them with positive and empowering affirmations. For example, replace "I'm not attractive enough" with "I am beautiful and deserving of love." Repeat these affirmations daily to rewire your mindset and boost your confidence.

Setting Realistic Goals

Setting realistic goals is an important part of building confidence and assertiveness. When it comes to dating, it's essential to set goals that align with your values and desires. Take some time to reflect on what you truly want in a partner and a relationship. What are your non-negotiables? What qualities are important to you? By setting clear and realistic goals, you will have a better understanding of what you're looking for, which will increase your confidence in navigating the dating scene.

Stepping Out of Your Comfort Zone

Building confidence and assertiveness often requires stepping out of your comfort zone. It's natural to feel nervous or anxious when trying new things or meeting new people, but growth happens outside of our comfort zones. Challenge yourself to engage in activities or events that align with your interests and values. This could be joining LGBTQ+ social groups, attending community events, or participating in hobbies that you enjoy. By pushing yourself to try new experiences, you will not only expand your social circle but also boost your confidence in social settings.

Practicing Self-Care

Self-care plays a crucial role in building confidence and assertiveness. Taking care of your physical, emotional, and mental well-being is essential for feeling confident and empowered. Make self-care a priority in your daily routine. This could include activities such as exercise, meditation, journaling, or spending time with loved ones. When you prioritize self-care, you send a message to yourself and others that you value your well-being, which in turn boosts your confidence.

Developing Assertiveness Skills

Assertiveness is the ability to express your thoughts, feelings, and needs in a clear and respectful manner. Developing assertiveness skills is crucial for healthy communication and setting boundaries in relationships. Practice assertiveness by expressing your opinions and needs in everyday situations. Start with small steps, such as speaking up in group discussions or politely declining invitations that don't align with your interests. As you become more comfortable with assertiveness, you will feel more confident in expressing your needs and desires in your dating life.

Building a Supportive Network

Surrounding yourself with a supportive network of friends, family, and like-minded individuals is essential for building confidence and assertiveness. Seek out people who uplift and encourage you in your journey. Engage in conversations and activities that align with your values and interests. Having a supportive network not only boosts your confidence but also provides a safe space to share your experiences and seek advice when needed.

Celebrating Your Successes

Finally, remember to celebrate your successes along the way. Building confidence and assertiveness is a journey, and it's important to acknowledge and celebrate your progress. Whether it's going on a successful date, setting a boundary, or stepping out of your comfort zone, take the time to recognize and celebrate your achievements. By celebrating your successes, you reinforce positive behaviors and build a strong foundation of confidence and assertiveness.

Building confidence and assertiveness takes time and practice, but with dedication and self-reflection, you can cultivate these essential skills. Remember, confidence is attractive, and assertiveness is necessary for healthy relationships. Embrace who you are, challenge your limiting beliefs, and step out of your comfort zone. By doing so, you will not only enhance your dating experience but also create a life filled with confidence, empowerment, and love.

2

Chapter 2

Navigating the Dating Scene

2.1 Setting Dating Goals

Setting clear and intentional dating goals is an essential step in finding the right partner. When you have a clear vision of what you want in a relationship, it becomes easier to navigate the dating scene and attract compatible partners. In this section, we will explore the importance of setting dating goals and provide you with practical tips on how to define and prioritize your relationship aspirations.

Why Set Dating Goals?

Setting dating goals allows you to approach the dating process with purpose and intention. It helps you avoid wasting time and energy on relationships that are not aligned with your values and desires. By defining your goals, you create a roadmap for yourself, guiding you towards the kind of relationship you truly desire.

Defining Your Dating Goals

To set effective dating goals, it is important to take the time to reflect on your desires, values, and priorities. Here are some steps to help you define your dating goals:

1. **Self-Reflection:** Start by reflecting on your past relationships and experiences. What worked well? What didn't? What are the qualities and values that are important to you in a partner? Understanding your own needs and desires is crucial in setting meaningful dating goals.
2. **Identify Deal Breakers:** Consider the qualities or behaviors that are non-negotiable for you in a relationship. These deal breakers could be related to values, communication styles, or lifestyle choices. Knowing your deal breakers will help you filter out potential partners who are not compatible with your core values.
3. **Prioritize Your Goals:** Once you have identified your desires and deal breakers, prioritize them based on their importance to you. This will help you focus on the aspects that matter most in a relationship and avoid getting distracted by less significant factors.
4. **Be Realistic:** While it is important to have high standards and not settle for less than you deserve, it is also crucial to be realistic in your dating goals. Consider what is realistically attainable and sustainable in a relationship, keeping in mind that no one is perfect.
5. **Flexibility and Openness:** While having clear goals is important, it is also essential to remain open and flexible

to unexpected opportunities and connections. Sometimes, the right partner may come in a different package than you initially imagined. Stay open to possibilities while staying true to your core values.

Types of Dating Goals

Dating goals can vary from person to person, depending on individual preferences and relationship aspirations. Here are some common types of dating goals that you may consider:

1. **Finding a Life Partner:** If your ultimate goal is to find a long-term committed relationship or marriage, your dating goals may revolve around finding a partner who shares your values, goals, and vision for the future.
2. **Exploring Casual Dating:** If you are not ready for a serious commitment or are looking to explore different connections, your dating goals may involve meeting new people, having fun experiences, and learning more about yourself and others.
3. **Building Emotional Intimacy:** If you prioritize emotional connection and intimacy, your dating goals may focus on developing deep and meaningful connections with potential partners.
4. **Exploring Sexual Compatibility:** If sexual compatibility is important to you, your dating goals may involve exploring physical intimacy and finding partners who align with your desires and preferences.
5. **Personal Growth and Self-Discovery:** If personal growth and self-discovery are your priorities, your dating goals may involve meeting diverse individuals who can challenge

and inspire you to grow as a person.

Remember, your dating goals can evolve and change over time as you gain more clarity about what you truly want in a relationship. It is important to regularly reassess and adjust your goals as you learn and grow through the dating process.

Putting Your Goals into Action

Once you have defined your dating goals, it's time to put them into action. Here are some practical tips to help you align your dating experiences with your goals:

1. **Communicate Your Intentions:** Be clear and upfront about your dating goals when communicating with potential partners. This will help you attract individuals who are on the same page and avoid misunderstandings.
2. **Choose the Right Dating Platforms:** Select dating platforms or communities that align with your dating goals. Whether it's online dating apps, LGBTQ+ events, or social groups, choose platforms that attract individuals who share similar relationship aspirations.
3. **Be Selective:** Don't feel pressured to date everyone who shows interest in you. Be selective and choose partners who align with your goals and values. Quality over quantity is key.
4. **Take Your Time:** Avoid rushing into relationships. Take the time to get to know potential partners and assess their compatibility with your goals. Remember, it's okay to take things slow and prioritize your own well-being.
5. **Regularly Reassess:** Regularly reassess your dating goals

to ensure they still align with your evolving desires and values. As you grow and learn, your goals may change, and that's perfectly normal.

By setting clear dating goals and aligning your actions with them, you increase your chances of finding a partner who is compatible with your desires and aspirations. Remember, dating is a journey of self-discovery, and setting conscious goals will help you navigate this journey with clarity and intention.

2.2 Creating an Authentic Dating Profile

Creating an authentic dating profile is an essential step in navigating the dating scene as a conscious lesbian. Your dating profile serves as your first impression and can greatly impact the type of connections you make. By crafting a profile that reflects your true self, you increase your chances of attracting compatible partners who align with your values and desires. In this section, we will explore the key elements of creating an authentic dating profile that showcases your uniqueness and attracts the right people.

2.2.1 Choosing the Right Platform

Before diving into the details of your dating profile, it's important to choose the right platform that aligns with your dating goals and values. There are various dating apps and websites available, each with its own user base and features. Take some time to research and select a platform that caters to the lesbian community and promotes inclusivity and respect. Look for platforms that prioritize safety and have a positive reputation within the LGBTQ+ community.

2.2.2 Showcasing Your Personality

When creating your dating profile, it's crucial to showcase your personality authentically. Start by writing a captivating bio that highlights your interests, hobbies, and values. Be specific and genuine in describing yourself, as this will help attract individuals who resonate with your unique qualities. Avoid generic statements and clichés, and instead, focus on sharing what makes you truly special.

Consider including anecdotes or stories that reflect your passions and experiences. This will not only give potential matches a glimpse into your life but also provide them with conversation starters. Remember, the goal is to create a profile that stands out and sparks curiosity.

2.2.3 Choosing the Right Photos

Selecting the right photos for your dating profile is crucial in making a positive first impression. Your photos should accurately represent who you are and what you enjoy doing. Include a variety of pictures that showcase different aspects of your life, such as hobbies, travel, or social activities. Avoid using heavily filtered or overly edited photos, as they can create unrealistic expectations.

It's also important to include clear and recent photos of yourself. Choose images where you feel confident and comfortable, as this will attract individuals who appreciate your authentic self. Consider asking a friend to help you choose the best photos or seek professional assistance if needed.

2.2.4 Honesty and Transparency

When creating your dating profile, it's essential to be honest and transparent about your intentions and expectations. Clearly communicate what you are looking for in a partner and what you bring to the table. This will help filter out individuals who may not align with your goals or values, saving both parties time and potential heartache.

Avoid exaggerating or misrepresenting yourself in any way. Honesty is the foundation of building meaningful connections, and starting off with a lie can lead to disappointment and mistrust. Be proud of who you are and embrace your uniqueness. Remember, the right person will appreciate and value you for who you truly are.

2.2.5 Embracing Inclusivity

As a conscious lesbian, it's important to create a dating profile that embraces inclusivity and respects the diversity within the LGBTQ+ community. Use inclusive language and avoid making assumptions or generalizations about others. Be open-minded and willing to learn from different perspectives.

When describing your preferences, be mindful of not perpetuating stereotypes or excluding certain groups. Embrace the beauty of diversity and be open to connecting with individuals from various backgrounds and experiences. By fostering inclusivity in your dating profile, you increase your chances of attracting a diverse range of potential partners.

2.2.6 Seeking Feedback and Making Adjustments

Creating an authentic dating profile is an ongoing process. It's important to seek feedback from trusted friends or mentors who can provide constructive criticism. They can help you identify areas for improvement and offer suggestions on how to better showcase your personality and values.

Regularly review and update your dating profile to ensure it accurately represents who you are at different stages of your life. As you grow and evolve, your dating preferences and goals may change, and it's important to reflect these changes in your profile. Remember, your dating profile is a reflection of your journey and the person you are becoming.

Creating an authentic dating profile is an opportunity to showcase your true self and attract compatible partners who appreciate and value you. By being genuine, transparent, and inclusive, you increase your chances of finding meaningful connections that align with your desires and values. Embrace the process and have fun exploring the possibilities that await you in the dating world.

2.3 Finding Compatible Partners

Finding a compatible partner is an essential step in lesbian dating and building a fulfilling relationship. When searching for a potential partner, it's important to approach the process with intention and consciousness. This section will guide you through the process of finding compatible partners by exploring self-awareness, understanding your preferences, and navigating the dating scene.

Understanding Your Preferences

Before embarking on the journey of finding a compatible partner, it's crucial to have a clear understanding of your preferences and what you are looking for in a relationship. Take some time to reflect on your values, interests, and goals. Consider the qualities and characteristics that are important to you in a partner. This self-reflection will help you identify the type of person you are most compatible with and ensure that you are seeking a relationship that aligns with your needs and desires.

Defining Compatibility

Compatibility is the foundation of a successful and fulfilling relationship. It goes beyond shared interests and physical attraction. Compatibility involves emotional, intellectual, and spiritual alignment. It's about finding someone who complements your strengths and weaknesses, shares similar values and goals, and supports your personal growth.

To determine compatibility, it's important to consider various aspects of a potential partner, such as their communication style, emotional intelligence, and ability to handle conflict. Assess whether their values and beliefs align with yours and if they have a similar vision for the future. Compatibility is not about finding someone who is exactly like you, but rather someone who complements and enhances your life.

Expanding Your Social Circle

One effective way to increase your chances of finding compatible partners is to expand your social circle. Engage in activities and join communities that align with your interests and values. Attend LGBTQ+ events, join social clubs, or participate in online forums and groups. By surrounding yourself with like-minded individuals, you increase the likelihood of meeting someone who shares your passions and values.

Networking within the LGBTQ+ community can also provide opportunities to meet potential partners. Attend local pride events, join LGBTQ+ organizations, or volunteer for causes that are important to you. These spaces not only allow you to connect with potential partners but also provide a supportive and inclusive environment where you can be your authentic self.

Online Dating

In today's digital age, online dating has become a popular and convenient way to meet potential partners. There are numerous dating platforms specifically designed for the LGBTQ+ community, offering a safe and inclusive space to connect with like-minded individuals.

When creating an online dating profile, be authentic and transparent about who you are and what you are looking for. Highlight your interests, values, and goals to attract potential partners who align with your preferences. Take the time to read through profiles and engage in meaningful conversations to assess compatibility before meeting in person.

While online dating can be a valuable tool, it's important to approach it with caution. Be mindful of your safety and take necessary precautions when meeting someone for the first time. Trust your instincts and prioritize your well-being throughout the process.

Seeking Support from Friends and Community

Your friends and community can be valuable resources in finding compatible partners. They may have connections or be aware of individuals who share similar interests and values. Don't hesitate to reach out to your friends and let them know that you are actively seeking a compatible partner. They may be able to introduce you to someone who could be a potential match.

Additionally, consider joining support groups or seeking guidance from LGBTQ+ organizations. These spaces provide a supportive community where you can share experiences, seek advice, and potentially meet individuals who are also looking for compatible partners.

Trusting the Process

Finding a compatible partner takes time and patience. It's important to trust the process and not settle for someone who doesn't align with your values and goals. Remember that compatibility is essential for a healthy and fulfilling relationship. Be open to new experiences, learn from each interaction, and trust that the right person will come into your life when the time is right.

By understanding your preferences, expanding your social circle, utilizing online dating platforms, seeking support from friends and community, and trusting the process, you increase your chances of finding compatible partners. Remember to approach the dating journey with consciousness and intention, and always prioritize your own well-being and happiness.

2.4 Effective Communication and Connection

Effective communication is the cornerstone of any successful relationship, and lesbian dating is no exception. In order to build a strong connection with your partner, it is crucial to develop healthy communication skills that foster understanding, empathy, and mutual respect. This section will explore various strategies and techniques to enhance communication and connection in your lesbian relationships.

2.4.1 Active Listening

One of the most important aspects of effective communication is active listening. This means giving your partner your full attention and genuinely seeking to understand their perspective. When your partner is speaking, avoid interrupting or formulating your response in your mind. Instead, focus on what they are saying and try to empathize with their feelings and experiences. Reflect back on what they have said to ensure that you have understood correctly. Active listening not only helps you understand your partner better but also shows them that you value their thoughts and feelings.

2.4.2 Open and Honest Communication

Open and honest communication is essential for building trust and intimacy in a lesbian relationship. It involves expressing your thoughts, feelings, and needs in a clear and respectful manner. Avoid making assumptions or expecting your partner to read your mind. Instead, communicate openly about your desires, boundaries, and expectations. Be willing to listen to your partner's perspective and validate their feelings. Remember that effective communication is a two-way street, and both partners should feel comfortable expressing themselves without fear of judgment or criticism.

2.4.3 Non-Verbal Communication

Non-verbal communication plays a significant role in how we connect with others. Pay attention to your body language, facial expressions, and tone of voice when communicating with your partner. Non-verbal cues can convey emotions and intentions that words alone may not capture. Maintain eye contact, use open and inviting body language, and be aware of your tone of voice. Non-verbal cues can either enhance or hinder effective communication, so strive to align your non-verbal signals with your verbal messages to create a sense of trust and understanding.

2.4.4 Conflict Resolution

Conflict is a natural part of any relationship, and how you handle it can either strengthen or weaken your connection. When conflicts arise, it is important to approach them with a mindset of resolution rather than winning. Practice active listening and empathy to understand your partner's perspective. Avoid blaming or criticizing and instead focus on expressing your feelings and needs using "I" statements. Collaborate with your partner to find mutually beneficial solutions and be willing to compromise. Remember that conflicts can be opportunities for growth and deeper understanding if approached with respect and open-mindedness.

2.4.5 Emotional Intelligence

Emotional intelligence is the ability to recognize, understand, and manage your own emotions, as well as the emotions of others. Developing emotional intelligence can greatly enhance your communication and connection with your partner. Take the time to reflect on your own emotions and understand how they may influence your communication style. Practice empathy by putting yourself in your partner's shoes and trying to understand their emotions and experiences. Validate their feelings and respond with compassion and understanding. By cultivating emotional intelligence, you can create a safe and supportive space for open and honest communication.

2.4.6 Cultivating Connection

Building a strong connection with your partner requires ongoing effort and intention. Make time for regular check-ins and conversations to deepen your understanding of each other. Engage in activities that foster connection, such as shared hobbies, date nights, or weekend getaways. Show appreciation for your partner and express gratitude for their presence in your life. Small gestures of love and affection can go a long way in maintaining a strong connection. Remember that connection is not just about talking but also about actively listening, understanding, and supporting each other.

2.4.7 Seeking Professional Help

Sometimes, despite our best efforts, communication challenges persist. In such cases, seeking professional help can be beneficial. A therapist or relationship counselor can provide guidance and tools to improve communication and connection in your lesbian relationship. They can help you navigate through difficult conversations, manage conflicts, and develop effective communication strategies. Seeking professional help is a sign of strength and commitment to the growth and success of your relationship.

In conclusion, effective communication and connection are vital for building and maintaining a healthy lesbian relationship. By practicing active listening, open and honest communication, and emotional intelligence, you can foster a deep and meaningful connection with your partner. Remember that communication is a skill that can be developed and improved over time. With patience, understanding, and a commitment to growth, you can create a strong foundation for love and connection in your lesbian relationships.

3

Chapter 3

Building Healthy Relationships

3.1 Establishing Boundaries and Consent

Establishing boundaries and consent is a crucial aspect of building healthy and fulfilling relationships. As a conscious lesbian dater, it is essential to prioritize your own needs and desires while respecting those of your partner. By setting clear boundaries and practicing enthusiastic consent, you can create a safe and respectful space for both yourself and your partner to explore and grow together.

Understanding Boundaries

Boundaries are the limits we set for ourselves in terms of what we are comfortable with, both physically and emotionally. They define our personal space, values, and expectations within a relationship. Understanding and communicating your boundaries is essential for maintaining a healthy and respectful connection with your partner.

To establish your boundaries, take some time to reflect on your values, needs, and comfort levels. Consider what you are willing to engage in and what you are not comfortable with. It is important to remember that boundaries can change over time, so regular self-reflection and open communication with your partner are key.

Communicating Boundaries

Once you have a clear understanding of your boundaries, it is crucial to communicate them effectively to your partner. Open and honest communication is the foundation of any healthy relationship. When discussing boundaries, it is important to be assertive and direct while maintaining respect and empathy.

Start by having a conversation with your partner about boundaries. Clearly express what you are comfortable with and what you are not. Use "I" statements to avoid sounding accusatory or judgmental. For example, instead of saying, "You always invade my personal space," say, "I feel uncomfortable when my personal space is invaded."

Encourage your partner to share their boundaries as well. Listen actively and without judgment, and be willing to compromise and find common ground. Remember that boundaries are not about controlling or restricting your partner but about creating a safe and respectful space for both of you.

Respecting Boundaries

Respecting your partner's boundaries is just as important as setting your own. It is essential to honor and acknowledge their limits and preferences. When your partner communicates their boundaries, make a conscious effort to understand and respect them.

Respecting boundaries also means seeking enthusiastic consent in all aspects of your relationship. Consent should be freely given, enthusiastic, and ongoing. It is important to check in with your partner regularly and ensure that they are comfortable and willing to engage in any activity. Remember that consent can be withdrawn at any time, and it is crucial to respect your partner's decision.

Navigating Challenging Situations

In any relationship, there may be times when boundaries are tested or crossed unintentionally. It is important to address these situations with open communication and empathy. If you feel that your boundaries have been violated, express your concerns to your partner in a calm and non-confrontational manner.

Listen to your partner's perspective and try to understand their intentions. Sometimes, misunderstandings or miscommunications can occur, and it is important to give each other the benefit of the doubt. However, if your boundaries continue to be disregarded or if your partner shows a lack of respect for your limits, it may be necessary to reevaluate the relationship.

Seeking Professional Help

If you find it challenging to establish or communicate your boundaries, or if you are struggling with a partner who consistently disrespects your limits, seeking professional help can be beneficial. A therapist or counselor who specializes in relationships can provide guidance and support in navigating these issues.

Remember, establishing boundaries and practicing consent is an ongoing process. As you grow and evolve as individuals and as a couple, your boundaries may change. Regularly check in with yourself and your partner to ensure that your boundaries are being respected and that you are both feeling safe and fulfilled in the relationship. By prioritizing open communication, empathy, and respect, you can create a strong foundation for a healthy and conscious lesbian relationship.

3.2 Managing Conflict and Resolving Issues

Conflict is a natural part of any relationship, and learning how to effectively manage and resolve conflicts is crucial for building a healthy and lasting partnership. In this section, we will explore strategies and techniques for managing conflict and resolving issues in your lesbian relationships.

Understanding Conflict

Conflict arises when there is a disagreement or clash of interests between two individuals. It can stem from differences in values, beliefs, needs, or desires. It is important to recognize that conflict is not inherently negative; in fact, it can be an opportunity for growth and deeper understanding within a relationship.

Open and Honest Communication

One of the key foundations for managing conflict is open and honest communication. It is essential to create a safe and non-judgmental space where both partners can express their thoughts, feelings, and concerns. Active listening is crucial during these conversations, as it allows each partner to feel heard and understood.

When conflicts arise, it is important to avoid blaming or attacking your partner. Instead, focus on using "I" statements to express your own feelings and needs. For example, instead of saying, "You never listen to me," try saying, "I feel unheard when I share my thoughts and ideas."

Identifying the Root Cause

To effectively resolve conflicts, it is important to identify the root cause of the issue. Often, conflicts are not just about the surface-level disagreement but are rooted in deeper underlying issues. Take the time to reflect on what might be triggering the conflict and explore any patterns or recurring themes that may be present.

Finding Common Ground

In any conflict, it is important to find common ground and areas of agreement. This can help create a sense of unity and collaboration, rather than focusing solely on the differences.

Look for shared values or goals that can serve as a foundation for finding a resolution.

Seeking Compromise

Compromise is an essential part of resolving conflicts. It involves finding a middle ground where both partners can feel satisfied with the outcome. It is important to approach compromise with a mindset of collaboration rather than competition. Remember that compromise does not mean sacrificing your own needs or values; it is about finding a solution that honors both partners' perspectives.

Active Problem-Solving

When conflicts arise, it can be helpful to engage in active problem-solving. This involves breaking down the issue into smaller, manageable parts and brainstorming potential solutions. Encourage creativity and open-mindedness during this process. Consider seeking outside perspectives or professional help if needed.

Taking Responsibility

In conflict resolution, it is important for each partner to take responsibility for their own actions and contributions to the conflict. This involves acknowledging any mistakes or shortcomings and being willing to make amends. Taking responsibility also means being accountable for your own emotions and reactions during conflicts.

Practicing Forgiveness

Forgiveness is a powerful tool for resolving conflicts and healing wounds within a relationship. It involves letting go of resentment and choosing to move forward with love and compassion. Forgiveness does not mean forgetting or condoning harmful behavior, but rather releasing the negative emotions associated with the conflict.

Seeking Professional Help

In some cases, conflicts may be too complex or deeply rooted to be resolved solely through personal efforts. Seeking the help of a professional therapist or counselor can provide valuable guidance and support in navigating conflicts. A trained professional can help facilitate open and productive communication, provide tools for conflict resolution, and offer a neutral perspective.

Conclusion

Conflict is an inevitable part of any relationship, but it does not have to be destructive. By approaching conflicts with open communication, empathy, and a willingness to find common ground, you can effectively manage and resolve issues in your lesbian relationships. Remember that conflict can be an opportunity for growth and deeper connection if approached with consciousness and a commitment to mutual understanding.

3.3 Nurturing Emotional Intimacy

Emotional intimacy is a vital aspect of any healthy and fulfilling relationship. It involves creating a deep connection with your partner, where you feel safe, understood, and supported. Nurturing emotional intimacy requires effort, communication, and vulnerability. In this section, we will explore various strategies and practices to help you cultivate and maintain emotional intimacy in your lesbian relationships.

1. Cultivating Open and Honest Communication

Open and honest communication is the foundation of emotional intimacy. It involves expressing your thoughts, feelings, and needs to your partner in a respectful and non-judgmental manner. To nurture emotional intimacy, it is essential to create a safe space where both partners feel comfortable sharing their innermost thoughts and emotions.

Here are some tips for cultivating open and honest communication:

- Practice active listening: Give your partner your full attention when they are speaking. Show empathy and understanding by reflecting back what they have said and asking clarifying questions.
- Use "I" statements: When expressing your feelings or concerns, use "I" statements to avoid sounding accusatory. For example, say "I feel hurt when..." instead of "You always make me feel..."
- Be vulnerable: Share your fears, dreams, and insecurities with your partner. Vulnerability fosters trust and deepens

emotional connection.

- Regular check-ins: Set aside dedicated time to have open and honest conversations about your relationship. Discuss any concerns, desires, or changes you would like to make together.

2. Building Trust and Emotional Safety

Trust is the cornerstone of emotional intimacy. It is crucial to create an environment where both partners feel safe to be themselves and share their true selves without fear of judgment or betrayal. Building trust takes time and consistent effort. Here are some ways to build trust and emotional safety:

- Keep your promises: Follow through on your commitments and be reliable. This helps your partner feel secure and builds trust.
- Be consistent: Consistency in your words and actions helps your partner feel safe and secure in the relationship.
- Respect boundaries: Honor your partner's boundaries and communicate your own. Respecting boundaries fosters trust and shows that you value and care for each other's emotional well-being.
- Be transparent: Share important information and be open about your thoughts and feelings. Honesty and transparency build trust and deepen emotional intimacy.

3. Practicing Empathy and Understanding

Empathy is the ability to understand and share the feelings of another person. It is a powerful tool for nurturing emotional intimacy. When you practice empathy, you create a deeper connection with your partner by truly understanding their experiences and emotions.

Here are some ways to practice empathy and understanding:

- Validate emotions: Acknowledge and validate your partner's emotions, even if you don't fully understand them. Let them know that their feelings are valid and important to you.
- Put yourself in their shoes: Try to see things from your partner's perspective. This helps you understand their experiences and respond with empathy.
- Ask open-ended questions: Encourage your partner to share more about their thoughts and feelings by asking open-ended questions. This shows that you are genuinely interested in understanding them.
- Show compassion: Be compassionate and supportive when your partner is going through a difficult time. Offer comfort and reassurance, and let them know that you are there for them.

4. Engaging in Meaningful Activities Together

Engaging in meaningful activities together can deepen emotional intimacy by creating shared experiences and memories. These activities can be as simple as cooking a meal together, going for a walk, or pursuing a shared hobby or interest.

Here are some ideas for meaningful activities:

- Take a weekend getaway: Plan a trip together to explore new places and create lasting memories.
- Volunteer together: Engaging in community service or volunteering can strengthen your bond as you work towards a common goal.
- Create rituals: Establish rituals or traditions that are unique to your relationship. This could be a weekly date night, a monthly adventure, or a yearly celebration of your love.

5. Expressing Love and Affection

Expressing love and affection is essential for nurturing emotional intimacy. Small gestures of love and appreciation can go a long way in strengthening your connection with your partner.

Here are some ways to express love and affection:

- Physical touch: Hug, kiss, hold hands, and cuddle with your partner. Physical touch releases oxytocin, a hormone that promotes bonding and emotional connection.
- Words of affirmation: Express your love and appreciation through kind and supportive words. Let your partner know how much they mean to you and how grateful you are to have them in your life.
- Acts of service: Show your love by doing something thoughtful for your partner. It could be cooking their favorite meal, running errands for them, or surprising them with a small gift.
- Quality time: Dedicate quality time to be fully present with your partner. Put away distractions and engage in activities

that you both enjoy.

Remember, nurturing emotional intimacy is an ongoing process that requires effort and commitment from both partners. By practicing open communication, building trust, showing empathy, engaging in meaningful activities, and expressing love and affection, you can create a deep and fulfilling emotional connection with your partner.

3.4 Maintaining Trust and Honesty

Trust and honesty are the foundation of any healthy and successful relationship. In the context of lesbian dating and love, maintaining trust and honesty becomes even more crucial. As two women navigate the complexities of their connection, it is essential to establish a strong sense of trust and maintain open and honest communication. This section will explore the importance of trust and honesty in lesbian relationships and provide practical tips on how to cultivate and sustain these qualities.

The Importance of Trust

Trust is the cornerstone of any relationship. It is the belief that your partner is reliable, dependable, and has your best interests at heart. In a lesbian relationship, trust is vital because it allows both partners to feel safe, secure, and emotionally connected. Trust enables you to be vulnerable with your partner, knowing that they will respect and honor your feelings and boundaries.

Without trust, a relationship can become strained and filled with doubt and insecurity. It is essential to establish trust early on and nurture it throughout the relationship. Here are some key aspects to consider when it comes to building and maintaining trust:

1. Consistency and Reliability

Consistency and reliability are crucial in building trust. It means showing up for your partner consistently, being reliable in your actions and words, and following through on your commitments. When you consistently demonstrate your trustworthiness, your partner will feel secure in the relationship.

2. Open and Honest Communication

Open and honest communication is the foundation of trust. It involves sharing your thoughts, feelings, and concerns with your partner without fear of judgment or rejection. When both partners communicate openly and honestly, it fosters a sense of trust and deepens the emotional connection.

3. Respect for Boundaries

Respecting each other's boundaries is essential for building trust. It means honoring your partner's limits and not crossing them without their consent. Respecting boundaries shows that you value and trust your partner's autonomy and individuality.

4. Trusting Your Intuition

Trusting your intuition is an important aspect of maintaining trust. If something feels off or raises concerns, it is crucial to address it openly and honestly with your partner. Trusting your intuition allows you to address potential issues before they escalate and impact the trust in your relationship.

Cultivating Honesty

Honesty is the bedrock of trust. It involves being truthful, transparent, and authentic in your words and actions. Cultivating honesty in your relationship requires vulnerability and a commitment to open communication. Here are some strategies to help you cultivate honesty in your lesbian relationship:

1. Practice Self-Reflection

Self-reflection is an essential tool for cultivating honesty. Take the time to reflect on your own thoughts, feelings, and motivations. Understand your own biases, fears, and insecurities, as they can impact your ability to be honest with your partner. By being aware of your own inner landscape, you can approach your relationship with greater honesty and authenticity.

2. Create a Safe Space for Honesty

Creating a safe space for honesty is crucial in a lesbian relationship. Both partners should feel comfortable expressing their thoughts and feelings without fear of judgment or reprisal. Foster an environment of trust and acceptance where both partners can be vulnerable and share their truth openly.

3. Practice Active Listening

Active listening is a powerful tool for cultivating honesty. It involves fully engaging with your partner when they are speaking, giving them your undivided attention, and validating their feelings. By actively listening, you create a space for your partner to be honest and open, strengthening the bond of trust between you.

4. Be Accountable and Take Responsibility

Honesty also means being accountable for your actions and taking responsibility for any mistakes or shortcomings. When you make a mistake, own up to it, apologize sincerely, and take steps to rectify the situation. Being accountable shows your partner that you value honesty and are committed to maintaining trust in the relationship.

Overcoming Challenges to Trust and Honesty

Maintaining trust and honesty in a lesbian relationship can sometimes be challenging. External factors such as past traumas, insecurities, or societal pressures can impact the trust between partners. Here are some strategies to overcome these challenges:

1. Seek Professional Help

If trust and honesty become significant challenges in your relationship, seeking the help of a professional therapist or counselor can be beneficial. They can provide guidance and support in navigating the complexities of trust and honesty and help you develop strategies to overcome any obstacles.

2. Practice Self-Care

Taking care of yourself is essential in maintaining trust and honesty. Engage in activities that promote self-care and self-reflection, such as meditation, journaling, or engaging in hobbies you enjoy. When you prioritize your well-being, you are better equipped to show up authentically and honestly in your relationship.

3. Communicate and Reassure

If trust issues arise, it is crucial to communicate openly and honestly with your partner. Share your concerns, fears, and insecurities, and work together to find solutions. Reassure your partner of your commitment to the relationship and your dedication to maintaining trust and honesty.

4. Practice Patience and Understanding

Building and maintaining trust takes time and effort. Be patient with yourself and your partner as you navigate the complexities of trust and honesty. Understand that trust is a continuous process and that it may require ongoing work and communication to sustain.

In conclusion, trust and honesty are fundamental pillars of a healthy and fulfilling lesbian relationship. By prioritizing open communication, respecting boundaries, and practicing self-reflection, you can cultivate and maintain trust and honesty in your relationship. Remember that trust is built through consistency, reliability, and vulnerability, and honesty is fostered through active listening, accountability, and creating a safe space for open communication. With these foundations in place, you can create a strong and lasting connection with your partner based on trust and honesty.

3.5 Supporting Each Other's Growth

In any healthy and fulfilling relationship, it is essential to support each other's growth. This means being there for your partner as they navigate their personal journey of self-discovery, self-improvement, and personal development. Supporting each other's growth not only strengthens the bond between you but also allows both individuals to thrive and become the best versions of themselves.

3.5.1 Encouraging Personal Goals and Dreams

One of the ways to support each other's growth is by encouraging and nurturing each other's personal goals and dreams. As individuals, we all have unique aspirations and ambitions that contribute to our overall happiness and fulfillment. By actively supporting and cheering on your partner's dreams, you create an environment of love, trust, and encouragement.

Take the time to listen to your partner's goals and dreams, and show genuine interest and enthusiasm. Offer words of encouragement, provide emotional support, and be their biggest cheerleader. Celebrate their achievements and milestones along the way, and be there to offer a helping hand when needed. By actively supporting each other's personal goals and dreams, you create a strong foundation for growth and success within your relationship.

3.5.2 Providing Emotional Support

Emotional support is a crucial aspect of supporting each other's growth. Life can be challenging at times, and having a partner who is there to provide a listening ear, a shoulder to lean on, and a safe space to express emotions can make a world of difference. As a conscious lesbian couple, it is important to create an environment where both partners feel comfortable opening up and sharing their feelings.

Practice active listening when your partner is expressing their emotions. Validate their feelings and let them know that you are there for them. Offer words of comfort and reassurance, and avoid judgment or criticism. Sometimes, all someone needs is a compassionate and understanding presence to help them navigate through difficult times.

3.5.3 Challenging Each Other to Grow

Supporting each other's growth also means challenging each other to step outside of your comfort zones and embrace personal growth. Growth often happens when we push ourselves beyond our limits and explore new possibilities. As a couple, you can encourage each other to take risks, try new experiences, and pursue personal development opportunities.

Engage in open and honest conversations about your individual goals and areas for growth. Encourage each other to take on new challenges and offer support and guidance along the way. Be each other's accountability partner, holding each other responsible for personal growth and development. By challenging each other to grow, you create a dynamic and evolving relationship that fosters continuous improvement.

3.5.4 Respecting Individual Paths

While supporting each other's growth is important, it is equally crucial to respect and honor each other's individual paths. Each person's journey of self-discovery and personal development is unique, and it is essential to recognize and embrace these differences.

Respecting individual paths means allowing your partner the space and freedom to explore their own interests, passions, and personal growth opportunities. Avoid imposing your own expectations or desires onto your partner's journey. Instead, offer support and encouragement as they navigate their own path.

3.5.5 Celebrating Milestones and Achievements

As you support each other's growth, it is important to celebrate the milestones and achievements along the way. Whether it's a small victory or a significant accomplishment, taking the time to acknowledge and celebrate each other's successes strengthens the bond between you.

Celebrate your partner's milestones with genuine joy and excitement. Plan special dates or surprises to commemorate their achievements. By celebrating each other's growth and accomplishments, you create a positive and uplifting atmosphere within your relationship.

3.5.6 Seeking Growth Together

While individual growth is important, seeking growth together as a couple can also be a powerful way to support each other's development. Explore opportunities for shared learning, personal development workshops, or couples' therapy. Engage in activities that promote growth and self-improvement as a team.

By actively seeking growth together, you create a strong foundation for personal and relational development. This shared commitment to growth strengthens your bond and allows you to evolve and thrive as a couple.

In conclusion, supporting each other's growth is a vital aspect of a conscious lesbian relationship. Encouraging personal goals and dreams, providing emotional support, challenging each other to grow, respecting individual paths, celebrating milestones, and seeking growth together are all essential components of supporting each other's growth. By actively supporting and nurturing each other's personal development, you create a relationship that fosters growth, happiness, and fulfillment for both partners.

3.6 Balancing Independence and Togetherness

Finding the right balance between independence and togetherness is crucial in any relationship, and lesbian relationships are no exception. As individuals, we all have our own needs for personal space, autonomy, and independence. At the same time, we also crave connection, intimacy, and shared experiences with our partners. Balancing these two aspects can be challenging, but with conscious effort and open communication, it is possible to create a healthy and fulfilling dynamic.

Understanding Independence and Togetherness

Independence refers to the ability to maintain your own identity, pursue your own interests, and have a sense of self outside of the relationship. It is about having the freedom to make decisions and choices that align with your values and desires. On the other hand, togetherness is about building a strong bond with your partner, sharing experiences, and creating a sense of unity and partnership.

It is important to recognize that independence and togetherness are not mutually exclusive. In fact, they can complement each other and contribute to the overall strength of the relationship. When both partners have a healthy level of independence, it allows for personal growth, self-discovery, and a sense of fulfillment. At the same time, togetherness provides emotional support, companionship, and a shared sense of purpose.

Communicating Needs and Boundaries

The key to balancing independence and togetherness lies in open and honest communication. It is essential to express your needs, desires, and boundaries to your partner. This includes discussing how much alone time you require, what activities you enjoy doing independently, and what activities you prefer to do together. By having these conversations, you can ensure that both partners feel heard, understood, and respected.

It is also important to establish boundaries that honor each partner's need for independence. This may involve setting aside specific times for personal hobbies or interests, respecting each other's personal space, and allowing for individual growth and exploration. By clearly defining these boundaries, you can avoid feelings of suffocation or neglect and create a healthy balance between independence and togetherness.

Cultivating Individuality

Maintaining a sense of individuality is crucial in any relationship. It is important to continue pursuing your own passions, interests, and goals, even when in a committed partnership. This not only allows for personal growth but also brings new experiences and perspectives into the relationship.

Encourage your partner to explore their own interests and support them in their endeavors. Celebrate each other's achievements and provide a safe space for personal expression. By nurturing individuality, you can create a strong foundation for a healthy and balanced relationship.

Quality Time Together

While independence is important, it is equally important to prioritize quality time together. This means setting aside dedicated time to connect, communicate, and engage in shared activities. Quality time allows for emotional intimacy, deepens the bond between partners, and strengthens the foundation of the relationship.

Plan regular date nights, weekend getaways, or even simple activities like cooking together or going for a walk. Use this time to truly connect with each other, share your thoughts and feelings, and create lasting memories. By making quality time a priority, you can nurture the togetherness in your relationship.

Supporting Each Other's Independence

In a healthy relationship, both partners should actively support and encourage each other's independence. This means celebrating each other's achievements, providing emotional support during challenging times, and respecting each other's decisions and choices.

Encourage your partner to pursue their dreams and goals, even if it means spending time apart or making sacrifices. Be their biggest cheerleader and offer a helping hand whenever needed. By supporting each other's independence, you can create a strong sense of trust, respect, and admiration within the relationship.

Reassessing and Adjusting

Balancing independence and togetherness is an ongoing process that requires regular reassessment and adjustment. As individuals grow and evolve, their needs and desires may change. It is important to have open and honest conversations with your partner to ensure that both of you are still aligned in terms of your expectations and boundaries.

Regularly check in with each other to discuss how you are feeling in the relationship and if any adjustments need to be made. Be open to compromise and find creative solutions that allow both partners to feel fulfilled and supported.

Conclusion

Balancing independence and togetherness is a delicate dance in any relationship, and conscious effort is required to maintain a healthy equilibrium. By understanding and communicating your needs, cultivating individuality, prioritizing quality time together, and supporting each other's independence, you can create a strong and fulfilling partnership. Remember, finding the right balance is a journey, and it may require ongoing adjustments as you and your partner grow and evolve together.

4

Chapter 4

Exploring Intimacy and Sexuality

4.1 Understanding Sexual Orientation and Identity

Understanding your sexual orientation and identity is a crucial aspect of conscious lesbian dating and love. It forms the foundation of your self-awareness and helps you navigate the dating world with confidence and authenticity. In this section, we will explore the concept of sexual orientation, the different dimensions of identity, and how they influence your dating experiences.

What is Sexual Orientation?

Sexual orientation refers to a person's enduring pattern of emotional, romantic, and sexual attractions to individuals of the same gender, different gender, or both genders. It is an intrinsic part of who you are and plays a significant role in shaping your relationships and experiences. For lesbians, sexual orientation involves a primary attraction to other women.

Dimensions of Identity

Sexual orientation is just one aspect of your overall identity. It is important to recognize that identity is multifaceted and can encompass various dimensions, including gender identity, gender expression, and cultural or ethnic background. Understanding these dimensions can help you embrace your authentic self and foster meaningful connections with others.

Gender Identity: Gender identity refers to how you perceive and experience your own gender. It is about your internal sense of being male, female, or something else. For lesbians, gender identity aligns with being female.

Gender Expression: Gender expression relates to how you present your gender to others through behavior, clothing, and personal style. It is a way of expressing your identity and can vary along a spectrum from masculine to feminine or androgynous. Remember that there is no right or wrong way to express your gender as a lesbian. Embrace your unique expression and let it shine.

Cultural and Ethnic Background: Your cultural and ethnic background adds another layer to your identity. It influences your values, beliefs, and traditions, which can impact your dating preferences and experiences. Embracing your cultural heritage and sharing it with your partner can deepen your connection and create a richer relationship.

Fluidity and Exploration

Sexual orientation and identity are not fixed or static. They can evolve and change over time as you gain new insights and experiences. It is essential to give yourself permission to explore and discover who you are without judgment or pressure. This exploration can involve questioning your attractions, experimenting with different labels, or embracing a fluid identity that allows for flexibility and growth.

Remember that your journey of self-discovery is unique to you. It is okay to take your time and explore at your own pace. Surround yourself with supportive and understanding individuals who can provide guidance and encouragement along the way.

Labels and Identity

Labels can be both empowering and limiting. While they can provide a sense of belonging and community, they can also create expectations and stereotypes. It is important to remember that labels are tools for self-identification, not boxes that define who you are entirely.

As a lesbian, you may choose to identify with the label "lesbian" or prefer other terms such as "gay," "queer," or "sapphic." The label you choose is a personal decision and should reflect your authentic self. It is also important to respect and honor the labels that others choose for themselves.

Intersectionality and Inclusivity

Understanding sexual orientation and identity requires acknowledging the intersectionality of identities. Intersectionality recognizes that individuals can experience multiple forms of oppression or privilege based on their race, ethnicity, socioeconomic status, disability, and other factors. It is crucial to approach dating and relationships with an inclusive mindset that values and respects the diverse experiences of others.

By embracing intersectionality, you can foster a more inclusive and compassionate dating environment. Educate yourself about the experiences of lesbians from different backgrounds and actively seek out diverse perspectives. This will not only enrich your own understanding but also contribute to a more inclusive and supportive community.

Conclusion

Understanding your sexual orientation and identity is an ongoing process that requires self-reflection, exploration, and acceptance. By embracing your authentic self and recognizing the diverse dimensions of your identity, you can navigate the dating world with confidence and attract partners who appreciate and value you for who you are. Remember, your sexual orientation and identity are beautiful aspects of your being, and they deserve to be celebrated and respected.

4.2 Exploring Sexual Compatibility

Sexual compatibility is an essential aspect of any romantic relationship, and it plays a significant role in the overall satisfaction and longevity of the partnership. When it comes to lesbian dating, understanding and exploring sexual compatibility can be a transformative experience that deepens the connection between partners. In this section, we will delve into the various factors that contribute to sexual compatibility and provide guidance on how to navigate this aspect of your relationship.

Understanding Sexual Compatibility

Sexual compatibility refers to the degree to which partners' sexual desires, preferences, and needs align with each other. It encompasses a wide range of factors, including physical attraction, sexual interests, communication, and emotional intimacy. It is important to note that sexual compatibility is not solely determined by physical attraction but also by emotional and psychological factors.

To explore sexual compatibility, it is crucial to have open and honest conversations with your partner about your desires, boundaries, and expectations. This requires creating a safe and non-judgmental space where both partners can express themselves freely. By discussing your sexual needs and desires, you can gain a deeper understanding of each other's preferences and work towards finding a mutually satisfying sexual dynamic.

Communicating About Sexual Desires

Effective communication is the cornerstone of exploring sexual compatibility. It is essential to openly discuss your desires, fantasies, and boundaries with your partner. This can be done through open-ended questions, active listening, and non-verbal cues. By actively engaging in these conversations, you can create an environment of trust and understanding, allowing both partners to feel comfortable expressing their needs and desires.

It is important to remember that sexual desires can evolve and change over time. Regular check-ins with your partner can help ensure that both of you are still satisfied and fulfilled in your sexual relationship. By maintaining open lines of communication, you can address any concerns or desires that may arise and work together to find solutions that meet both partners' needs.

Exploring Sexual Fantasies and Experimentation

Exploring sexual fantasies and engaging in experimentation can be a powerful way to enhance sexual compatibility. By sharing your fantasies with your partner, you can create a space where both of you feel comfortable exploring new experiences together. It is crucial to approach these discussions with an open mind and a willingness to listen and understand your partner's desires.

Experimentation can involve trying new positions, incorporating sex toys, or exploring different forms of sexual play. However, it is important to establish clear boundaries and consent before engaging in any new activities. Consent should always be enthusiastic, ongoing, and freely given by all parties involved.

Addressing Differences in Sexual Desire

It is common for partners to have different levels of sexual desire or libido. If you find that you and your partner have differing levels of sexual desire, it is important to approach this issue with empathy and understanding. Open and honest communication is key in addressing these differences and finding a solution that works for both partners.

One approach to addressing differences in sexual desire is to explore alternative forms of intimacy and connection. This can involve engaging in non-sexual activities that foster emotional closeness and intimacy, such as cuddling, holding hands, or engaging in deep conversations. By focusing on emotional intimacy, you can maintain a strong connection with your partner even if your sexual desires do not always align.

Seeking Professional Help

If you and your partner are struggling to navigate sexual compatibility issues, seeking the guidance of a professional can be beneficial. A sex therapist or relationship counselor can provide a safe and supportive environment for both partners to explore their sexual desires, address any concerns, and develop strategies for enhancing sexual compatibility.

Remember, sexual compatibility is not a fixed state but an ongoing process of exploration and understanding. It requires open communication, empathy, and a willingness to adapt and grow together. By actively engaging in these conversations and prioritizing each other's needs, you can create a fulfilling and satisfying sexual relationship that strengthens your overall connection as a couple.

4.3 Enhancing Intimacy and Connection

Intimacy and connection are vital aspects of any romantic relationship, and they play an especially important role in lesbian relationships. As a conscious lesbian dater, you understand the significance of fostering a deep emotional bond and creating a strong connection with your partner. In this section, we will explore various ways to enhance intimacy and connection in your relationship.

1. Prioritize Emotional Intimacy

Emotional intimacy forms the foundation of a strong and fulfilling relationship. It involves sharing your thoughts, feelings, and vulnerabilities with your partner, and creating a safe space for them to do the same. To enhance emotional intimacy:

- Practice active listening: Give your partner your full attention when they are speaking, and make an effort to understand their perspective without judgment. Reflect back on what they say to show that you are truly listening and validating their feelings.
- Express empathy and understanding: Show your partner that you empathize with their experiences and emotions. Validate their feelings and let them know that you are there to support them unconditionally.
- Share your own emotions: Openly express your own feelings

and thoughts with your partner. This vulnerability will encourage them to do the same, deepening the emotional connection between you.

2. Cultivate Physical Intimacy

Physical intimacy is an essential component of a romantic relationship. It involves not only sexual intimacy but also non-sexual touch, affection, and closeness. To enhance physical intimacy:

- Engage in non-sexual touch: Physical touch, such as holding hands, hugging, cuddling, or giving massages, can create a sense of closeness and comfort. Make an effort to incorporate non-sexual touch into your daily interactions.
- Explore sexual desires and fantasies: Communicate openly with your partner about your sexual desires and fantasies. Discuss what brings you pleasure and explore new experiences together, ensuring that both partners feel comfortable and respected.
- Prioritize sexual satisfaction: Pay attention to your partner's sexual needs and desires, and communicate your own. Experiment with different techniques, positions, or activities to keep the sexual aspect of your relationship exciting and fulfilling.

3. Foster Intellectual Connection

An intellectual connection involves engaging in stimulating conversations, sharing common interests, and supporting each other's intellectual growth. To enhance intellectual connection:

- Engage in meaningful conversations: Discuss topics that interest both of you, such as current events, books, movies, or personal goals. Ask open-ended questions and actively listen to your partner's thoughts and opinions.
- Explore new interests together: Discover new hobbies or activities that you both enjoy. This shared experience will not only deepen your connection but also create lasting memories.
- Support each other's intellectual growth: Encourage your partner to pursue their passions and interests. Share resources, recommend books or articles, and engage in discussions that challenge and inspire both of you.

4. Nurture Spiritual Connection

Spiritual connection goes beyond religious beliefs and involves connecting on a deeper level, sharing values, and finding meaning together. To enhance spiritual connection:

- Share your beliefs and values: Discuss your spiritual beliefs, values, and what gives your life meaning. Find common ground and explore ways to align your values and goals.
- Engage in spiritual practices together: Participate in activities that nurture your spiritual connection, such as meditation, yoga, or attending religious or spiritual gatherings. These shared experiences can deepen your bond and create a sense of unity.
- Support each other's spiritual growth: Encourage your partner's spiritual journey and provide support as they explore their beliefs. Respect each other's individual paths and be open to learning from one another.

5. Practice Mindful Presence

Being fully present with your partner is crucial for enhancing intimacy and connection. To practice mindful presence:

- Put away distractions: When spending quality time with your partner, put away your phone, turn off the TV, and eliminate any other distractions. Give them your undivided attention and create a space for deep connection.
- Practice active appreciation: Express gratitude and appreciation for your partner regularly. Acknowledge their efforts, strengths, and the positive impact they have on your life. This practice fosters a sense of love and connection.
- Engage in shared activities: Find activities that you both enjoy and make time for them regularly. Whether it's cooking together, going for walks, or engaging in a shared hobby, these activities create opportunities for bonding and connection.

By prioritizing emotional intimacy, cultivating physical intimacy, fostering intellectual and spiritual connection, and practicing mindful presence, you can enhance the intimacy and connection in your lesbian relationship. Remember that building and maintaining a strong connection requires ongoing effort and communication. Embrace the journey of deepening your bond with your partner and enjoy the rewards of a fulfilling and loving relationship.

4.4 Navigating Sexual Health and Safety

Sexual health and safety are important aspects of any intimate relationship, including lesbian relationships. As a conscious lesbian dater, it is crucial to prioritize your sexual well-being and take proactive steps to ensure a safe and enjoyable sexual experience. This section will provide you with valuable information and guidance on navigating sexual health and safety in your relationships.

Understanding Sexual Health

Sexual health encompasses more than just the absence of disease; it includes physical, emotional, and social well-being in relation to sexuality. As a conscious lesbian dater, it is essential to have a comprehensive understanding of sexual health and its various aspects.

Regular Check-ups and Screenings

Regular check-ups and screenings are vital for maintaining good sexual health. Schedule routine visits with your healthcare provider to discuss any concerns, receive necessary vaccinations, and undergo screenings for sexually transmitted infections (STIs). Regular check-ups can help detect and treat any potential health issues early on.

Safe Sex Practices

Practicing safe sex is crucial for protecting yourself and your partner(s) from STIs. While lesbian sexual activity carries a lower risk of certain STIs, it is still important to take precautions. Here are some safe sex practices to consider:

- Use dental dams or latex barriers during oral sex to reduce the risk of STIs.

- Use condoms on sex toys and change them between partners or activities.
- Regularly clean sex toys with warm water and mild soap or use toy-specific cleaners.
- Avoid sharing sex toys unless they can be properly sterilized or covered with a condom.
- Consider getting vaccinated against STIs such as human papillomavirus (HPV) and hepatitis B.

Consent and Communication

Consent and communication are fundamental aspects of sexual health and safety. It is essential to establish clear boundaries and obtain enthusiastic consent from your partner(s) before engaging in any sexual activity. Consent should be ongoing and can be withdrawn at any time. Open and honest communication about desires, boundaries, and expectations is key to ensuring a safe and pleasurable sexual experience for everyone involved.

Preventing and Managing STIs

While practicing safe sex significantly reduces the risk of contracting STIs, it is important to be aware of the common infections that can affect lesbian women. Here are some STIs to be mindful of:

Human Papillomavirus (HPV)

HPV is a common viral infection that can be transmitted through skin-to-skin contact, including genital contact. It can lead to genital warts and certain types of cancer. Vaccination against HPV is available and recommended for all individuals, regardless of sexual orientation.

Bacterial Vaginosis (BV)

BV is a common vaginal infection caused by an imbalance of bacteria in the vagina. It can cause symptoms such as abnormal discharge, itching, and odor. While BV is not considered a sexually transmitted infection, it can be triggered by sexual activity. Maintaining good vaginal hygiene and avoiding douching can help prevent BV.

Yeast Infections

Yeast infections, also known as candidiasis, are caused by an overgrowth of yeast in the vagina. They can cause itching, burning, and abnormal discharge. While yeast infections are not typically considered sexually transmitted, they can be triggered by sexual activity. Avoiding excessive moisture, wearing breathable underwear, and practicing good hygiene can help prevent yeast infections.

Regular Testing and Treatment

Regular STI testing is essential for maintaining sexual health. Talk to your healthcare provider about the recommended testing schedule based on your sexual activity and individual risk factors. If you or your partner(s) test positive for an STI, seek treatment promptly and follow the prescribed course of action to prevent further transmission.

Emotional Well-being and Intimacy

Sexual health is not just about physical well-being; it also encompasses emotional well-being and intimacy. Here are some important considerations for nurturing emotional well-being in your sexual relationships:

Open Communication

Maintaining open and honest communication with your partner(s) about your sexual desires, boundaries, and concerns is crucial for fostering emotional intimacy. Create a safe space where you can discuss your needs and desires without judgment or shame.

Emotional Connection

Building emotional connection and intimacy outside of the bedroom can enhance your sexual experiences. Engage in activities that promote emotional bonding, such as spending quality time together, engaging in deep conversations, and expressing love and appreciation for each other.

Mutual Respect and Consent

Respecting each other's boundaries and obtaining consent before engaging in any sexual activity is essential for emotional well-being. Prioritize your partner's comfort and ensure that both of you feel safe and respected throughout your sexual encounters.

Seeking Support and Resources

Navigating sexual health and safety can sometimes feel overwhelming. Remember that you are not alone, and there are resources available to support you. Consider the following options:

Healthcare Providers

Consulting with healthcare providers who specialize in LGBTQ+ healthcare can provide you with tailored guidance and support. They can address any specific concerns you may have and offer appropriate advice and resources.

LGBTQ+ Community Organizations

Local LGBTQ+ community organizations often provide resources, workshops, and support groups focused on sexual health and well-being. These organizations can connect you with like-minded individuals and provide a safe space to discuss your experiences and concerns.

Online Resources

Numerous online resources offer information and support on sexual health and safety for lesbian women. Websites, forums, and blogs dedicated to LGBTQ+ health can provide valuable insights and guidance.

Remember, sexual health and safety are ongoing processes that require continuous attention and care. By prioritizing your sexual well-being, practicing safe sex, and nurturing emotional intimacy, you can create a fulfilling and healthy sexual relationship with your partner(s).

5

Chapter 5

Overcoming Challenges

5.1 Dealing with Homophobia and Discrimination

Homophobia and discrimination are unfortunate realities that many LGBTQ+ individuals face in their daily lives. As a lesbian, it is important to be prepared for the challenges that may arise due to societal prejudices. This section will provide you with guidance on how to navigate and cope with homophobia and discrimination in your dating and love life.

Understanding Homophobia and Discrimination

Homophobia refers to the fear, hatred, or prejudice against individuals who identify as LGBTQ+. It can manifest in various forms, including verbal abuse, physical violence, exclusion, and discrimination. Discrimination, on the other hand, involves treating someone unfairly or differently based on their sexual orientation.

It is crucial to recognize that homophobia and discrimination are not a reflection of your worth or identity. They stem from ignorance, prejudice, and societal biases. By understanding this, you can better equip yourself to handle these challenges with resilience and self-assurance.

Building a Supportive Network

One of the most effective ways to deal with homophobia and discrimination is by surrounding yourself with a supportive network of friends, family, and community. Seek out individuals who accept and celebrate your identity as a lesbian. These allies can provide emotional support, guidance, and a safe space to express your feelings and experiences.

Consider joining LGBTQ+ support groups, attending pride events, or participating in community organizations that advocate for LGBTQ+ rights. These spaces can offer a sense of belonging and solidarity, allowing you to connect with others who have faced similar challenges.

Educating Yourself and Others

Education is a powerful tool in combating homophobia and discrimination. By educating yourself about LGBTQ+ history, rights, and experiences, you can become more confident in your own identity and better equipped to challenge misconceptions and stereotypes.

Share your knowledge with others, whether it be through conversations, social media, or participating in LGBTQ+ awareness campaigns. By raising awareness and promoting understanding, you can help break down barriers and foster acceptance.

Responding to Homophobic Remarks or Actions

Unfortunately, you may encounter homophobic remarks or actions from individuals who are ignorant or intolerant. It is important to remember that you have the right to defend yourself and set boundaries. However, it is equally important to prioritize your safety and well-being.

When faced with homophobia, consider the following strategies:

1. Stay Calm: Responding with anger or aggression may escalate the situation. Take a deep breath and remain composed.
2. Educate: If you feel comfortable, calmly explain why the remark or action is offensive or hurtful. Share your personal experiences or provide factual information to challenge misconceptions.
3. Disengage: If the situation becomes hostile or unsafe, it may be best to disengage and remove yourself from the situation. Your safety should always be the top priority.
4. Seek Support: Reach out to your support network for emotional support and guidance after experiencing homophobia. Talking to someone who understands can help you process your emotions and regain a sense of security.

Legal Rights and Resources

Familiarize yourself with the legal rights and protections available to LGBTQ+ individuals in your country or region. Understanding your rights can empower you to assert yourself and seek justice if you experience discrimination or harassment.

Additionally, research local LGBTQ+ organizations and resources that can provide legal advice, counseling, or assistance in navigating discriminatory situations. These organizations often have helplines or online resources that can offer guidance and support.

Self-Care and Emotional Well-being

Dealing with homophobia and discrimination can take a toll on your emotional well-being. It is essential to prioritize self-care and engage in activities that bring you joy and relaxation. This may include practicing mindfulness, engaging in hobbies, seeking therapy, or connecting with nature.

Remember to be kind to yourself and practice self-compassion. Surround yourself with positive influences and engage in activities that promote self-love and acceptance.

Conclusion

While homophobia and discrimination can be challenging, it is important to remember that you are not alone. By building a supportive network, educating yourself and others, responding assertively, and prioritizing self-care, you can navigate these obstacles with strength and resilience. Remember, your love and identity are valid, and you deserve to be treated with respect and acceptance.

5.2 Managing Long-Distance Relationships

Long-distance relationships can be challenging, but with conscious effort and effective communication, they can also be incredibly rewarding. In this section, we will explore strategies and tips for managing a long-distance relationship as a lesbian couple.

Understanding the Challenges

Being physically separated from your partner can present unique challenges in a relationship. It requires a strong commitment, trust, and open communication to make it work. Here are some common challenges you may face in a long-distance relationship:

1. **Distance and Lack of Physical Intimacy:** One of the most significant challenges in a long-distance relationship is the lack of physical intimacy. Being unable to hold hands, hug, or share physical affection can be difficult for any couple. It's important to find alternative ways to express love and affection, such as through video calls, sending care packages, or writing heartfelt letters.
2. **Communication and Time Zone Differences:** Long-distance relationships often involve navigating different time zones, which can make communication challenging. It's crucial to establish a communication routine that works for both of you. Set aside dedicated time for video calls or phone conversations, and make an effort to stay connected through texts or emails throughout the day.
3. **Loneliness and Emotional Strain:** Being physically apart

from your partner can lead to feelings of loneliness and emotional strain. It's important to acknowledge and validate these emotions while finding healthy ways to cope with them. Lean on your support system, engage in self-care activities, and maintain a positive mindset to help navigate these challenges.

Building Trust and Security

Trust is the foundation of any successful relationship, and it becomes even more crucial in a long-distance relationship. Here are some strategies to build trust and security:

1. **Open and Honest Communication:** Effective communication is key to building trust. Be open and honest with each other about your feelings, concerns, and expectations. Discuss any insecurities or fears you may have and work together to find solutions.
2. **Establishing Boundaries:** Establishing clear boundaries is essential in any relationship, but it becomes even more important in a long-distance relationship. Discuss and agree upon boundaries regarding communication, socializing, and personal space. Respecting each other's boundaries will help foster trust and security.
3. **Regular Check-Ins:** Regularly check in with each other to ensure that both partners feel secure and loved. This can be done through video calls, phone conversations, or even simple text messages. Regular check-ins help maintain a sense of connection and reassurance.

Making the Most of Visits

Visits are precious moments in a long-distance relationship, as they provide an opportunity to reconnect and strengthen your bond. Here are some tips for making the most of your visits:

1. **Plan Ahead:** Plan your visits in advance to ensure that both partners can make the necessary arrangements. Discuss and agree upon the duration of the visit, activities you want to do together, and any expectations you may have.
2. **Quality Time:** Make the most of your time together by prioritizing quality time. Engage in activities that you both enjoy, explore new places, and create lasting memories. Disconnect from distractions and focus on each other.
3. **Open Communication:** Use your visits as an opportunity to have open and honest conversations about the future of your relationship. Discuss your goals, aspirations, and plans for eventually closing the distance. It's important to be on the same page and have a shared vision for the future.

Utilizing Technology

Technology has made it easier than ever to stay connected in long-distance relationships. Here are some ways you can utilize technology to enhance your connection:

1. **Video Calls:** Video calls are a great way to see each other's faces and feel more connected. Schedule regular video calls to catch up, share your day, or simply spend time together virtually.

2. **Shared Activities:** Use technology to engage in shared activities, even when you're physically apart. Watch movies or TV shows together using streaming services, play online games, or even cook the same recipe simultaneously while video chatting.
3. **Virtual Dates:** Get creative with virtual dates. Plan a virtual dinner date where you both cook a meal and enjoy it together over video call. Or have a movie night where you synchronize watching a movie and discuss it afterward.

Maintaining Independence and Togetherness

Balancing independence and togetherness is crucial in any relationship, and it becomes even more important in a long-distance relationship. Here are some tips for maintaining a healthy balance:

1. **Pursue Individual Interests:** Use the time apart to pursue your individual interests and hobbies. This not only helps you grow as an individual but also gives you something to share and talk about with your partner.
2. **Support Each Other's Goals:** Encourage and support each other's personal and professional goals. Celebrate each other's achievements and provide emotional support when needed.
3. **Plan for the Future:** Have open and honest conversations about your future plans and goals as a couple. Discuss the possibility of eventually closing the distance and create a roadmap for how you will work towards that goal.

Remember, managing a long-distance relationship requires

patience, commitment, and effective communication. By implementing these strategies and maintaining a positive mindset, you can navigate the challenges and build a strong and fulfilling relationship, even from a distance.

5.3 Addressing Family and Social Acceptance

One of the most significant challenges that many lesbians face in their dating and love lives is the issue of family and social acceptance. While society has made great strides in LGBTQ+ rights and acceptance, there are still many individuals and communities that hold onto outdated beliefs and prejudices. This can make it difficult for lesbians to navigate their relationships and find the support they need from their loved ones.

Addressing family and social acceptance is a crucial step in creating a healthy and fulfilling relationship. It requires open communication, understanding, and sometimes, a willingness to educate and challenge the beliefs of those around you. In this section, we will explore strategies and tips for addressing family and social acceptance as a conscious lesbian dater.

1. Understand Your Own Journey

Before addressing family and social acceptance, it's essential to understand and accept your own journey. Recognize that your sexual orientation is a natural and beautiful part of who you are. Embrace your identity with confidence and self-love. When you are secure in your own truth, it becomes easier to navigate the challenges that may arise from others' lack of acceptance.

2. Choose the Right Time and Place

When it comes to addressing family and social acceptance, timing and environment are crucial. Choose a time and place where everyone involved can feel comfortable and open to discussion. It may be helpful to have a private conversation with family members or close friends who may have concerns or reservations about your relationship. This allows for a more intimate and personal conversation where you can express your feelings and answer any questions they may have.

3. Educate and Share Resources

Many individuals hold prejudices or misconceptions about LGBTQ+ relationships due to a lack of understanding or exposure. As a conscious lesbian dater, you can play a vital role in educating your loved ones and providing them with resources to learn more. Share books, articles, or documentaries that explore LGBTQ+ issues and relationships. Encourage them to engage in open-minded conversations and challenge their own beliefs.

4. Be Patient and Understanding

Addressing family and social acceptance is not always a one-time conversation. It may take time for your loved ones to process and accept your relationship fully. Be patient and understanding with their journey. Remember that their initial reactions may come from a place of fear or unfamiliarity. Give them space to ask questions, express concerns, and adjust to the new information.

5. Seek Support from LGBTQ+ Community

Finding support from the LGBTQ+ community can be incredibly empowering and helpful when addressing family and social acceptance. Connect with local LGBTQ+ organizations, support groups, or online communities where you can share your experiences and seek advice from others who have gone through similar situations. Surrounding yourself with a supportive network can provide you with the strength and resilience needed to navigate these challenges.

6. Set Boundaries and Protect Your Well-being

While it's important to address family and social acceptance, it's equally important to prioritize your own well-being. If you find yourself in toxic or unsupportive environments, it may be necessary to set boundaries or distance yourself from individuals who are not accepting of your relationship. Surround yourself with people who uplift and support you, even if they are not blood-related. Remember, your happiness and mental health should always be a priority.

7. Celebrate Your Love and Relationships

Despite the challenges, it's crucial to celebrate your love and relationships. Surround yourself with friends and loved ones who embrace and celebrate your relationship. Create a support system of individuals who uplift and validate your love. By focusing on the positive aspects of your relationship, you can counteract any negativity that may come from family or society.

8. Seek Professional Help if Needed

If you find that addressing family and social acceptance is causing significant distress or strain on your relationship, it may be beneficial to seek professional help. A therapist or counselor who specializes in LGBTQ+ issues can provide guidance and support as you navigate these challenges. They can help you develop coping strategies, improve communication skills, and find healthy ways to address any conflicts that arise.

Remember, addressing family and social acceptance is a journey that requires patience, understanding, and self-care. Surround yourself with a supportive network, educate those around you, and celebrate your love and relationships. By staying true to yourself and your values, you can create a fulfilling and authentic life, regardless of the acceptance of others.

5.4 Coping with Breakups and Heartbreak

Breakups and heartbreaks are an unfortunate reality of dating and relationships. No matter how conscious and intentional we are in our approach to love, sometimes things just don't work out. Coping with the end of a relationship can be incredibly challenging, especially when you have invested time, energy, and emotions into building a connection with someone. In this section, we will explore strategies and techniques to help you navigate the difficult process of coping with breakups and heartbreak.

Understanding the Grief Process

When a relationship ends, it is natural to experience a range of emotions. It is important to acknowledge and allow yourself to feel these emotions rather than suppressing them. The grief process is similar to mourning a loss, and it is essential to give yourself time and space to heal. Remember that healing is not linear, and everyone's journey is unique. Here are some stages you may go through during the grief process:

1. **Denial and Shock**: Initially, you may find it hard to accept that the relationship has ended. You might feel shocked and numb, unable to fully comprehend what has happened.
2. **Anger and Blame**: As reality sets in, you may start to feel anger towards your ex-partner or even yourself. It is important to acknowledge and express these emotions in healthy ways, such as through journaling, talking to a trusted friend, or seeking professional support.
3. **Bargaining**: During this stage, you may find yourself trying to negotiate with your ex-partner or making promises to change in the hope of getting back together. It is important to recognize that bargaining is a normal part of the grief process but ultimately may not lead to reconciliation.
4. **Sadness and Depression**: This stage is characterized by deep sadness and a sense of loss. It is crucial to allow yourself to grieve and seek support from loved ones or a therapist who can help you navigate these emotions.
5. **Acceptance and Moving On**: Eventually, with time and healing, you will reach a point of acceptance. You will begin to let go of the past and focus on building a brighter future for yourself.

Practicing Self-Care

During this challenging time, it is essential to prioritize self-care. Taking care of yourself physically, emotionally, and mentally will help you heal and move forward. Here are some self-care practices to consider:

1. **Allow Yourself to Feel**: Give yourself permission to experience the full range of emotions that come with a breakup. Cry, scream, or express your emotions in whatever way feels right for you. Remember that it is okay to not be okay.
2. **Take Time to Heal**: Healing takes time, and it is important to be patient with yourself. Avoid rushing into a new relationship or distracting yourself with unhealthy coping mechanisms. Instead, focus on self-reflection and personal growth.
3. **Practice Self-Compassion**: Be kind and gentle with yourself during this difficult time. Treat yourself with the same love and care you would offer a close friend. Practice positive self-talk and remind yourself that you deserve happiness and love.
4. **Engage in Activities that Bring You Joy**: Rediscover activities that bring you joy and make you feel alive. Whether it's spending time in nature, pursuing a hobby, or engaging in creative outlets, find ways to nourish your soul and reconnect with yourself.
5. **Seek Support**: Reach out to friends, family, or a therapist who can provide a listening ear and offer guidance. Surround yourself with a support system that understands and validates your feelings.

Reflecting and Learning

Breakups provide an opportunity for self-reflection and personal growth. Take this time to reflect on the relationship and learn from the experience. Here are some questions to guide your reflection:

1. **What Did I Learn from this Relationship?**: Reflect on the lessons you have learned from the relationship. Consider the positive aspects as well as the challenges you faced. Use these insights to grow and make better choices in future relationships.
2. **What Were My Contributions to the Breakup?**: Take responsibility for your part in the relationship's end. Reflect on your actions, behaviors, and patterns that may have contributed to the breakup. This self-awareness will help you avoid repeating the same mistakes in the future.
3. **What Are My Relationship Needs and Boundaries?**: Use this time to reassess your needs and boundaries in relationships. Consider what you want and deserve in a partner and what you are willing to compromise on. This reflection will help you make more conscious choices in your future dating endeavors.
4. **How Can I Grow from this Experience?**: Embrace the opportunity for personal growth and transformation. Use the lessons learned to become a stronger, more resilient individual. Focus on self-improvement and becoming the best version of yourself.

Moving Forward

Moving forward after a breakup can be challenging, but it is possible to find love and happiness again. Here are some tips to help you navigate this transition:

1. **Give Yourself Time**: Healing takes time, and it is important not to rush into a new relationship before you are ready. Take the time you need to heal and rediscover yourself.
2. **Focus on Self-Development**: Use this time to invest in your personal growth and development. Set goals, pursue new interests, and work on becoming the best version of yourself.
3. **Stay Open to New Opportunities**: While it is important to take time for yourself, don't close yourself off to new possibilities. Stay open to meeting new people and forming connections when you feel ready.
4. **Practice Gratitude**: Cultivate a sense of gratitude for the lessons learned and the experiences you had in the past relationship. Gratitude can help shift your perspective and bring positivity into your life.
5. **Seek Professional Help if Needed**: If you find it challenging to cope with the breakup on your own, consider seeking professional help. A therapist can provide guidance and support as you navigate the healing process.

Remember, breakups are a part of life, and while they may be painful, they also offer an opportunity for growth and self-discovery. By practicing self-care, reflecting on the experience, and moving forward with intention, you can heal and create a brighter future for yourself.

6

Chapter 6

Creating a Lasting Partnership

6.1 Building a Strong Foundation

Building a strong foundation is crucial for any lasting partnership, and lesbian relationships are no exception. When it comes to creating a solid base for your relationship, there are several key elements to consider. In this section, we will explore the importance of trust, communication, shared values, and emotional connection in building a strong foundation for your lesbian relationship.

Trust: The Bedrock of a Strong Relationship

Trust is the cornerstone of any successful relationship. It is the foundation upon which love, intimacy, and security are built. In a lesbian relationship, trust plays an even more significant role due to the unique challenges faced by the LGBTQ+ community. Building trust requires open and honest communication, consistency, and reliability.

To establish trust in your relationship, it is essential to be transparent with your partner. Share your thoughts, feelings, and fears openly, and encourage your partner to do the same. Be reliable and follow through on your commitments. Trust is not built overnight; it takes time and effort from both partners to cultivate a sense of security and faith in each other.

Effective Communication: The Key to Connection

Communication is the lifeblood of any relationship. It is through effective communication that partners can understand each other's needs, desires, and concerns. In a lesbian relationship, where two women may have different communication styles, it becomes even more important to find common ground and establish healthy communication patterns.

To build a strong foundation through communication, it is crucial to actively listen to your partner. Give them your full attention, validate their feelings, and respond with empathy. Avoid making assumptions and practice open-mindedness. Be willing to express your own needs and boundaries while respecting those of your partner. Regularly check in with each other to ensure that you are both on the same page and address any issues that may arise promptly.

Shared Values: Aligning Your Life Paths

Shared values are essential for a lasting partnership. While it is natural for individuals to have their own unique beliefs and values, finding common ground with your partner is crucial for building a strong foundation. Shared values provide a sense of unity, purpose, and direction in your relationship.

Take the time to discuss your core values with your partner. Explore topics such as family, career, spirituality, and personal growth. Identify areas where your values align and where there may be differences. It is important to respect each other's individuality while finding ways to integrate your shared values into your daily lives. This alignment will help you navigate challenges and make important decisions together.

Emotional Connection: The Heart of Intimacy

Emotional connection is the heart of intimacy in a lesbian relationship. It is the deep bond that allows partners to feel seen, heard, and understood. Building emotional connection requires vulnerability, empathy, and active engagement with your partner's emotions.

To foster emotional connection, create a safe space for open and honest expression of emotions. Practice empathy by putting yourself in your partner's shoes and seeking to understand their perspective. Show appreciation and gratitude for each other regularly. Engage in activities that promote emotional intimacy, such as deep conversations, shared hobbies, and quality time together. By nurturing emotional connection, you strengthen the foundation of your relationship.

Building a strong foundation in your lesbian relationship requires time, effort, and commitment from both partners. Trust, effective communication, shared values, and emotional connection are the pillars upon which a lasting partnership is built. By prioritizing these elements, you lay the groundwork for a fulfilling and loving relationship.

6.2 Planning for the Future

Planning for the future is an essential aspect of any relationship, and lesbian relationships are no exception. As you navigate the journey of conscious lesbian dating and love, it's important to consider your long-term goals and aspirations as a couple. This section will guide you through the process of planning for the future, helping you create a solid foundation for a lasting partnership.

Visualizing Your Future Together

One of the first steps in planning for the future is to visualize what you want your life together to look like. Take some time to imagine your ideal future as a couple. What are your dreams and aspirations? What kind of life do you envision for yourselves? This exercise will help you gain clarity and align your goals as a couple.

Setting Relationship Goals

Once you have a clear vision of your future, it's time to set relationship goals. Relationship goals are the milestones you want to achieve together as a couple. These goals can be both short-term and long-term and can encompass various aspects of your life, such as career, family, and personal growth. Setting goals will provide you with a sense of direction and purpose in your relationship.

When setting relationship goals, it's important to ensure that they are realistic and achievable. Consider your individual strengths and limitations, as well as the resources available to you. Discuss your goals openly and honestly with your partner, and make sure they align with both of your values and aspirations.

Financial Planning

Financial planning is a crucial aspect of planning for the future. It involves creating a budget, saving for major expenses, and making decisions about joint finances. As a couple, it's important to have open and honest conversations about money and establish a financial plan that works for both of you.

Consider discussing your financial goals and priorities. Are you planning to buy a house, start a business, or travel the world together? Determine how you will allocate your income, manage expenses, and save for the future. It's also important to discuss your individual financial responsibilities and how you will handle shared expenses.

Family Planning

For many couples, family planning is an important consideration for the future. As a lesbian couple, you may have different options and paths to explore when it comes to starting a family. Discuss your desires and expectations regarding children, and explore the various options available to you, such as adoption, surrogacy, or assisted reproductive technologies.

If you decide to have children, it's important to plan for the emotional, logistical, and financial aspects of parenting. Consider discussing your parenting styles, values, and expectations. Explore the support systems available to you, such as LGBTQ+ parenting groups and resources. Planning for the future as parents will help you navigate the journey of parenthood with confidence and preparedness.

Career and Personal Development

Planning for the future also involves considering your individual career and personal development goals. Discuss your professional aspirations and how they align with your life as a couple. Support each other's career growth and explore opportunities for personal development.

Consider how you can create a balance between your individual goals and your life as a couple. Discuss the possibility of pursuing joint ventures or supporting each other's entrepreneurial endeavors. Planning for the future should include space for personal growth and fulfillment, both as individuals and as a couple.

Reviewing and Revising Your Plans

As you progress in your relationship, it's important to regularly review and revise your plans for the future. Life is dynamic, and circumstances may change over time. Regularly check in with each other to ensure that your goals and aspirations are still aligned.

Be open to adjusting your plans as needed and be willing to compromise when necessary. Remember that planning for the future is an ongoing process, and it's important to adapt and grow together as a couple.

By planning for the future, you are creating a roadmap for your relationship. It allows you to align your goals, dreams, and aspirations, and build a solid foundation for a lasting partnership. Remember to communicate openly, be flexible, and support each other's growth as you navigate the exciting journey of conscious lesbian dating and love.

6.3 Creating Shared Values and Goals

In any relationship, shared values and goals play a crucial role in building a strong foundation and ensuring long-term compatibility. When it comes to lesbian dating and love, it becomes even more important to establish common ground and align your aspirations. Creating shared values and goals allows you and your partner to work towards a common vision, fostering a deeper connection and understanding. In this section, we will explore the significance of shared values and goals and provide guidance on how to create them within your relationship.

The Importance of Shared Values

Shared values act as a guiding compass for your relationship. They are the principles and beliefs that you and your partner hold dear and are essential for creating a harmonious and fulfilling partnership. When you share similar values, it becomes easier to navigate through life's challenges and make decisions together. It also helps in building trust and mutual respect, as you both understand and appreciate each other's perspectives.

When it comes to conscious lesbian dating and love, shared values become even more crucial. As members of the LGBTQ+ community, you may have experienced unique challenges and have specific needs and desires. Finding a partner who shares these values can provide a sense of validation, support, and understanding. It creates a safe space where you can be your authentic selves and grow together.

Identifying Your Values

Before you can create shared values with your partner, it is essential to identify and understand your own values. Take some time to reflect on what matters most to you in life. Consider your beliefs, principles, and the causes you are passionate about. Ask yourself questions like:

- What are my core values?
- What do I stand for?
- What are my non-negotiables in a relationship?
- What causes or issues am I passionate about?

By answering these questions, you will gain clarity on your values and what you bring to a relationship. It will also help you communicate your values effectively to your partner.

Communicating and Exploring Values with Your Partner

Once you have a clear understanding of your own values, it's time to communicate and explore them with your partner. Open and honest communication is key to creating shared values and goals. Here are some steps to guide you through the process:

1. **Create a safe space:** Find a comfortable and relaxed environment where you can have an open and honest conversation. Ensure that both you and your partner feel safe and respected during this discussion.

2. **Share your values:** Start by sharing your own values with your partner. Explain why these values are important to you and how they shape your life. Be open to listening to your partner's values as well, and show genuine interest and curiosity.
3. **Identify commonalities:** Look for areas where your values align. These shared values will form the foundation of your shared values and goals. Celebrate these commonalities and acknowledge the strength they bring to your relationship.
4. **Discuss differences:** It's natural to have some differences in values, and that's okay. Take the time to understand and respect each other's differing perspectives. Find ways to bridge the gap and create a space where both of your values can coexist harmoniously.
5. **Create shared goals:** Once you have identified your shared values, discuss and create goals that align with those values. These goals can be short-term or long-term and can encompass various aspects of your life, such as career, family, personal growth, or community involvement.
6. **Revisit and reassess:** As your relationship evolves, it's important to revisit and reassess your shared values and goals. Life circumstances may change, and new values may emerge. Regularly check in with each other to ensure that your shared values and goals continue to align with your evolving selves.

Nurturing Shared Values and Goals

Creating shared values and goals is just the beginning. Nurturing them requires ongoing effort and commitment from both partners. Here are some tips to help you nurture your shared values and goals:

1. **Regular communication:** Continuously communicate with your partner about your shared values and goals. Discuss any challenges or changes that may arise and find ways to address them together.
2. **Support each other:** Encourage and support each other in pursuing your shared goals. Be each other's cheerleaders and provide the necessary emotional support and motivation.
3. **Collaborate and compromise:** Remember that creating shared values and goals is a collaborative process. Be open to compromise and find middle ground when necessary. It's important to strike a balance between individual aspirations and shared dreams.
4. **Celebrate milestones:** Celebrate the milestones and achievements you reach together. Acknowledge the progress you have made towards your shared goals and use these moments to strengthen your bond.
5. **Revisit and revise:** Regularly revisit your shared values and goals to ensure they still resonate with both of you. As individuals and as a couple, you will grow and evolve, and it's important to adapt your shared values and goals accordingly.

By consciously creating shared values and goals, you and your partner can build a strong and fulfilling relationship. These shared values will serve as a solid foundation, guiding you through the ups and downs of life. Remember, it's not about finding someone who shares every single value, but rather finding someone who respects and supports your values while also having their own. Together, you can create a partnership that is grounded in love, understanding, and shared aspirations

6.4 Sustaining Passion and Romance

Sustaining passion and romance in a long-term lesbian relationship is essential for maintaining a deep connection and keeping the spark alive. As time goes on, it's natural for the initial excitement to fade, but with conscious effort and intention, you can continue to cultivate passion and romance in your relationship. In this section, we will explore some strategies and practices that can help you sustain the passion and keep the romance alive.

1. Prioritize Quality Time Together

One of the most effective ways to sustain passion and romance is by prioritizing quality time together. In the midst of busy lives, it's easy to get caught up in work, household chores, and other responsibilities, leaving little time for each other. However, making a conscious effort to spend quality time together is crucial.

Plan regular date nights or weekend getaways where you can focus solely on each other. Create a sacred space where you can connect emotionally, intellectually, and physically. This could be a cozy corner in your home, a favorite park, or a romantic restaurant. By dedicating uninterrupted time to each other, you can deepen your emotional bond and reignite the passion.

2. Keep the Element of Surprise Alive

Surprises can inject excitement and novelty into your relationship, helping to sustain passion and romance. Surprise your partner with small gestures of love and appreciation. It could be leaving a heartfelt note on their pillow, planning a surprise date, or organizing a weekend getaway without revealing the destination. These surprises show your partner that you are thinking of them and make them feel special.

Remember, surprises don't have to be extravagant or expensive. It's the thought and effort that counts. By keeping the element of surprise alive, you can create a sense of anticipation and keep the romance alive.

3. Explore New Experiences Together

Exploring new experiences together can reignite the passion and bring a sense of adventure into your relationship. Try new activities, hobbies, or travel to new places. Stepping out of your comfort zone and experiencing new things together can create shared memories and deepen your connection.

Consider taking a dance class, going on a hiking trip, or trying out a new cuisine. These shared experiences can bring you closer and create opportunities for passion and romance to flourish.

4. Communicate Openly and Honestly

Effective communication is the foundation of any successful relationship. To sustain passion and romance, it's important to communicate openly and honestly with your partner. Share your desires, fantasies, and needs with each other. Discuss your sexual preferences and explore ways to keep the intimacy alive.

Create a safe space where you can openly express your feelings and desires without judgment. By fostering open and honest communication, you can deepen your emotional connection and maintain a passionate and romantic relationship.

5. Prioritize Physical Intimacy

Physical intimacy plays a vital role in sustaining passion and romance. Make time for physical affection, such as cuddling, holding hands, and kissing. Physical touch releases oxytocin, the "love hormone," which strengthens the emotional bond between partners.

Explore different ways to keep the physical intimacy alive in your relationship. This could include trying new sexual experiences, experimenting with different techniques, or introducing toys or role-playing. Prioritize your sexual connection and make it a priority in your relationship.

6. Practice Gratitude and Appreciation

Expressing gratitude and appreciation for your partner is a powerful way to sustain passion and romance. Take time each day to acknowledge and appreciate the qualities you love about your partner. Express your gratitude for the little things they do for you.

By focusing on the positive aspects of your relationship and expressing your appreciation, you create a positive and loving atmosphere that fosters passion and romance.

7. Keep the Romance Alive Outside the Bedroom

Romance shouldn't be confined to the bedroom. Keep the romance alive in your everyday life by surprising your partner with small gestures of love and affection. Leave them a love note, send them a sweet text message, or prepare their favorite meal.

By infusing romance into your daily life, you create an atmosphere of love and connection that sustains passion and keeps the flame burning.

8. Continuously Explore Each Other's Desires

As individuals, we are constantly evolving, and so are our desires and needs. To sustain passion and romance, it's important to continuously explore each other's desires and fantasies. Have open and non-judgmental conversations about your sexual preferences and fantasies.

By staying curious and open-minded, you can create a safe space for both partners to express their desires and explore new experiences together.

9. Seek Support and Inspiration

Maintaining passion and romance in a long-term relationship can be challenging at times. Seek support and inspiration from other couples who have successfully sustained passion and romance in their relationships. Join online communities, attend workshops or retreats, or read books on maintaining passion and romance.

By learning from others and seeking inspiration, you can gather new ideas and strategies to keep the passion alive in your own relationship.

Remember, sustaining passion and romance requires conscious effort and intention. By prioritizing quality time together, keeping the element of surprise alive, exploring new experiences, communicating openly, prioritizing physical intimacy, practicing gratitude, and seeking support, you can create a lasting and passionate partnership.

7

Chapter 7

Self-Care and Personal Growth

7.1 Prioritizing Self-Care

Self-care is an essential aspect of maintaining a healthy and fulfilling life, especially when it comes to dating and relationships. As a conscious lesbian, it is crucial to prioritize self-care to ensure your own well-being and happiness. By taking care of yourself, you can show up as your best self in your relationships and create a strong foundation for love and connection. In this section, we will explore the importance of self-care and provide practical tips on how to prioritize it in your life.

The Importance of Self-Care

Self-care is not selfish; it is a necessary practice that allows you to recharge, rejuvenate, and nurture yourself. It involves taking deliberate actions to meet your physical, emotional, and mental needs. When you prioritize self-care, you are better equipped to handle the challenges that come with dating and relationships. Here are a few reasons why self-care is essential:

1. **Maintaining Balance:** Self-care helps you maintain a healthy balance between your personal life, dating, and relationships. It allows you to allocate time and energy to yourself, your partner, and other important aspects of your life.
2. **Enhancing Well-being:** Engaging in self-care activities promotes overall well-being. It helps reduce stress, anxiety, and burnout, allowing you to feel more grounded, centered, and content.
3. **Building Self-Worth:** Prioritizing self-care sends a powerful message to yourself and others that you value your own well-being. It helps build self-esteem and self-worth, which are essential for healthy relationships.
4. **Setting Boundaries:** Self-care involves setting boundaries and saying no when necessary. By prioritizing your needs, you establish healthy limits and prevent yourself from becoming overwhelmed or resentful.
5. **Modeling Healthy Behavior:** When you prioritize self-care, you become a role model for your partner and others around you. By demonstrating the importance of self-care, you encourage them to prioritize their own well-being as well.

Practical Tips for Prioritizing Self-Care

Now that we understand the significance of self-care, let's explore some practical tips for incorporating it into your daily life:

1. **Identify Your Needs:** Take some time to reflect on your needs and desires. What activities bring you joy and fulfillment? What helps you relax and recharge? By identifying your needs, you can create a self-care routine that aligns with your preferences.
2. **Create a Self-Care Plan:** Develop a self-care plan that includes activities you enjoy and that nourish your mind, body, and soul. This could include activities such as meditation, exercise, journaling, reading, spending time in nature, or engaging in creative pursuits. Schedule regular self-care activities into your calendar to ensure they become a priority.
3. **Practice Mindfulness:** Incorporate mindfulness into your self-care routine. Be fully present in the moment and engage in activities with intention and awareness. This can help you cultivate a sense of calm and reduce stress.
4. **Set Boundaries:** Learn to set boundaries and say no when necessary. It is okay to prioritize your own needs and decline invitations or requests that do not align with your self-care goals. Communicate your boundaries clearly and assertively.
5. **Nurture Your Relationships:** While self-care is about prioritizing yourself, it is also important to nurture your relationships. Make time for quality connections with your partner, friends, and loved ones. Engage in activities that strengthen your bond and bring you joy.
6. **Practice Self-Compassion:** Be kind and compassionate towards yourself. Treat yourself with the same love and care you would offer to a dear friend. Embrace self-acceptance and forgive yourself for any perceived shortcomings or mistakes.

7. **Seek Support:** Reach out for support when needed. Surround yourself with a supportive community of friends, family, or therapists who can provide guidance and encouragement. Remember, asking for help is a sign of strength, not weakness.
8. **Take Care of Your Physical Health:** Prioritize your physical health by engaging in regular exercise, eating nutritious foods, and getting enough restful sleep. Physical well-being is closely linked to mental and emotional well-being.
9. **Practice Self-Reflection:** Set aside time for self-reflection and introspection. Journaling, meditation, or engaging in therapy can help you gain insights into your thoughts, emotions, and patterns of behavior. This self-awareness can guide you in making conscious choices in your dating and relationship journey.

Remember, self-care is an ongoing practice that requires commitment and consistency. It is not a one-time event but a lifelong journey of self-discovery and self-nurturing. By prioritizing self-care, you are investing in your own well-being and creating a solid foundation for conscious lesbian dating and love.

7.2 Exploring Personal Development

Personal development is an essential aspect of our lives, regardless of our sexual orientation. It involves the continuous process of self-improvement, self-awareness, and self-growth. When it comes to lesbian dating and love, personal development plays a crucial role in creating a fulfilling and healthy relationship. It allows us to understand ourselves better, identify our strengths and weaknesses, and work towards becoming the best version of ourselves. In this section, we will explore the importance of personal development in the context of lesbian dating and love, and provide practical tips on how to embark on this journey.

The Importance of Personal Development

Personal development is the foundation for building a strong and lasting partnership. When we invest time and effort into our personal growth, we become more self-aware, confident, and emotionally resilient. This, in turn, positively impacts our relationships. Here are a few reasons why personal development is crucial in lesbian dating and love:

1. **Self-Awareness:** Personal development allows us to gain a deeper understanding of ourselves, including our values, beliefs, and desires. When we are aware of who we are and what we want, we can make conscious choices in our relationships.
2. **Emotional Intelligence:** Developing emotional intelligence helps us navigate the complexities of relationships. It involves understanding and managing our own emotions, as well as empathizing with our partner's feelings. By enhancing our emotional intelligence, we can communicate effectively, resolve conflicts, and foster intimacy.
3. **Self-Confidence:** Personal development boosts our self-confidence and self-esteem. When we feel good about ourselves, we are more likely to attract healthy and loving partners. Additionally, self-confidence allows us to set boundaries, express our needs, and assert ourselves in relationships.

4. **Growth Mindset:** Personal development encourages a growth mindset, which is essential for the success of any relationship. It involves embracing challenges, learning from failures, and continuously striving for improvement. By adopting a growth mindset, we can evolve as individuals and as a couple.

Embarking on the Personal Development Journey

Embarking on a personal development journey requires commitment, self-reflection, and a willingness to grow. Here are some practical tips to help you get started:

1. **Set Goals:** Start by setting personal development goals that align with your values and aspirations. These goals can be related to various aspects of your life, such as career, relationships, health, or spirituality. Write them down and create an action plan to achieve them.
2. **Self-Reflection:** Take time to reflect on your strengths, weaknesses, and areas for improvement. Journaling, meditation, or therapy can be helpful tools for self-reflection. Be honest with yourself and embrace self-acceptance. Remember, personal development is a journey, and it's okay to have areas that need growth.
3. **Continuous Learning:** Commit to lifelong learning and personal growth. Read books, attend workshops, or take courses that align with your interests and goals. Engage in activities that challenge you intellectually and emotionally. Surround yourself with people who inspire and support your personal development journey.
4. **Practice Self-Care:** Prioritize self-care as an integral part

of personal development. Take care of your physical, emotional, and mental well-being. Engage in activities that bring you joy, relaxation, and rejuvenation. This could include exercise, spending time in nature, practicing mindfulness, or engaging in creative pursuits.

5. **Seek Support:** Surround yourself with a supportive community of friends, mentors, or therapists who can provide guidance and encouragement. Share your personal development goals with them and seek their input and feedback. Having a support system can make the journey more enjoyable and fulfilling.
6. **Embrace Challenges:** Embrace challenges as opportunities for growth. Step out of your comfort zone and take on new experiences that push your boundaries. Whether it's trying a new hobby, taking on a leadership role, or confronting your fears, embracing challenges can lead to personal transformation.
7. **Celebrate Progress:** Celebrate your progress along the personal development journey. Acknowledge and appreciate the growth you have achieved. Celebrate milestones, big or small, and reward yourself for your efforts. This will motivate you to continue on the path of personal development.

Remember, personal development is a lifelong journey. It requires patience, perseverance, and self-compassion. As you continue to grow and evolve, you will not only enhance your own life but also create a strong foundation for a healthy and fulfilling relationship.

In the next section, we will explore the importance of finding balance in life and relationships. We will discuss strategies for maintaining a healthy equilibrium between personal growth, relationships, and other aspects of life.

7.3 Finding Balance in Life and Relationships

Finding balance in life and relationships is crucial for maintaining a healthy and fulfilling lesbian partnership. It involves creating harmony between various aspects of your life, such as work, personal growth, friendships, and your romantic relationship. When you achieve balance, you can navigate challenges with ease, nurture your own well-being, and cultivate a strong and lasting connection with your partner. In this section, we will explore strategies and practices that can help you find balance in your life and relationships.

Prioritizing Self-Care

One of the key elements of finding balance is prioritizing self-care. As a lesbian woman, it is essential to take care of your physical, emotional, and mental well-being. Self-care involves engaging in activities that bring you joy, relaxation, and rejuvenation. It can be as simple as taking a bubble bath, going for a walk in nature, practicing mindfulness or meditation, or indulging in a hobby you love.

Make self-care a non-negotiable part of your routine. Set aside dedicated time each day or week to focus on yourself and recharge. Remember that taking care of yourself is not selfish; it is necessary for your overall well-being and the health of your relationship. When you prioritize self-care, you have more energy and emotional capacity to invest in your partner and your relationship.

Balancing Work and Personal Life

Finding balance also means striking a healthy equilibrium between your work and personal life. In today's fast-paced world, it can be challenging to separate the two and avoid burnout. As a lesbian woman, it is important to create boundaries and establish clear lines between your professional responsibilities and personal time.

Set realistic expectations for yourself and communicate your boundaries with your employer, colleagues, and loved ones. Make sure to carve out time for activities that bring you joy and fulfillment outside of work. This could include spending quality time with your partner, engaging in hobbies, pursuing personal interests, or connecting with friends and family. By maintaining a healthy work-life balance, you can avoid feeling overwhelmed and ensure that your relationship receives the attention it deserves.

Cultivating Open Communication

Open and honest communication is the foundation of any healthy relationship. To find balance, it is crucial to cultivate effective communication with your partner. This involves actively listening to each other, expressing your needs and desires, and addressing any concerns or conflicts that arise.

Create a safe and non-judgmental space for open dialogue. Encourage your partner to share their thoughts and feelings, and be receptive to their perspective. Practice empathy and understanding, even when you may not agree on everything. By fostering open communication, you can strengthen your connection, resolve conflicts, and ensure that both partners feel heard and valued.

Setting Boundaries

Setting boundaries is an essential part of finding balance in life and relationships. Boundaries help define what is acceptable and what is not, ensuring that your needs and values are respected. As a lesbian woman, it is important to establish boundaries with your partner, friends, family, and even colleagues.

Reflect on your personal boundaries and communicate them clearly to your partner. Discuss what is comfortable and uncomfortable for you in various aspects of your relationship, such as personal space, alone time, social activities, and intimacy. Respect your partner's boundaries as well and work together to find a middle ground that honors both of your needs.

Nurturing Individual Growth

Finding balance in life and relationships also involves nurturing individual growth. As a lesbian woman, it is important to continue growing and evolving as an individual, even within the context of a partnership. Encourage your partner to pursue their passions, interests, and personal goals, and do the same for yourself.

Support each other's personal development by providing encouragement, space, and resources. Celebrate each other's achievements and milestones. By nurturing individual growth, you can maintain a sense of independence and personal fulfillment, which ultimately contributes to the health and longevity of your relationship.

Creating Quality Time Together

In the midst of busy lives, it is essential to create quality time for each other. Finding balance means dedicating uninterrupted time to connect, bond, and nurture your relationship. This could involve planning regular date nights, weekend getaways, or simply setting aside time each day to check in with each other.

During this quality time, focus on being present and fully engaged with your partner. Put away distractions such as phones or work-related tasks. Engage in activities that you both enjoy and that foster connection, such as cooking together, going for walks, or engaging in shared hobbies. By creating quality time together, you can deepen your emotional intimacy and strengthen your bond.

Embracing Flexibility

Lastly, finding balance in life and relationships requires embracing flexibility. Recognize that life is ever-changing, and your needs and priorities may shift over time. Be open to adapting your routines, expectations, and goals as necessary.

Embrace the ebb and flow of life and relationships. Be willing to compromise, negotiate, and adjust your plans when needed. By embracing flexibility, you can navigate the ups and downs of life with greater ease and maintain a sense of balance and harmony in your relationship.

Finding balance in life and relationships is an ongoing process. It requires self-reflection, open communication, and a commitment to nurturing both yourself and your partnership. By prioritizing self-care, setting boundaries, and embracing flexibility, you can create a strong foundation for a healthy and fulfilling lesbian relationship. Remember, finding balance is not about perfection but about continuously striving for harmony and growth.

7.4 Cultivating Happiness and Fulfillment

Finding happiness and fulfillment in life is a journey that requires self-reflection, self-care, and a commitment to personal growth. As a conscious lesbian dater, it is essential to prioritize your own happiness and well-being, as this will ultimately contribute to the success of your relationships. In this section, we will explore various strategies and practices that can help you cultivate happiness and fulfillment in your life.

Embracing Gratitude

One powerful way to cultivate happiness and fulfillment is by practicing gratitude. Gratitude is the practice of acknowledging and appreciating the positive aspects of your life. By focusing on what you are grateful for, you shift your perspective and invite more positivity into your life. Take a few moments each day to reflect on the things you are grateful for, whether it's the love and support of your partner, the beauty of nature, or the opportunities that come your way. Cultivating a gratitude practice can help you maintain a positive mindset and enhance your overall well-being.

Pursuing Passions and Hobbies

Engaging in activities that bring you joy and fulfillment is crucial for your overall happiness. Take the time to explore your passions and hobbies, whether it's painting, playing a musical instrument, writing, or participating in sports. When you engage in activities that you love, you tap into your creativity, boost your self-esteem, and experience a sense of fulfillment. Additionally, pursuing your passions can also provide opportunities to meet like-minded individuals who share your interests, potentially leading to new friendships or even romantic connections.

Nurturing Relationships and Connections

Building and maintaining meaningful relationships is an essential aspect of cultivating happiness and fulfillment. Surround yourself with people who uplift and support you, whether it's your partner, friends, or members of the LGBTQ+ community. Invest time and effort into nurturing these relationships, as they can provide a sense of belonging, love, and support. Engage in open and honest communication, practice active listening, and show appreciation for the people in your life. By fostering strong connections, you create a support system that can contribute to your overall happiness and well-being.

Practicing Mindfulness and Self-Reflection

Mindfulness is the practice of being fully present in the moment, without judgment. By cultivating mindfulness, you can develop a deeper understanding of yourself and your emotions. Take time each day to engage in mindfulness practices such as meditation, deep breathing exercises, or simply being fully present in your daily activities. This practice can help you become more aware of your thoughts, feelings, and desires, allowing you to make conscious choices that align with your values and bring you closer to happiness and fulfillment.

Self-reflection is another powerful tool for personal growth and happiness. Take regular moments to reflect on your experiences, relationships, and goals. Ask yourself meaningful questions such as "What brings me joy?" or "What areas of my life can I improve?" By engaging in self-reflection, you gain valuable insights into yourself and can make intentional choices that contribute to your overall happiness and fulfillment.

Cultivating Self-Compassion

Self-compassion is the practice of treating yourself with kindness, understanding, and acceptance. As a conscious lesbian dater, it is important to extend compassion to yourself, especially during challenging times. Be gentle with yourself and acknowledge that you are doing the best you can. Embrace self-care practices that nourish your mind, body, and soul, such as taking relaxing baths, practicing yoga, or engaging in activities that bring you joy. By cultivating self-compassion, you create a foundation of love and acceptance within yourself, which can positively impact your relationships and overall well-being.

Setting and Pursuing Meaningful Goals

Having goals that align with your values and aspirations can provide a sense of purpose and fulfillment. Take the time to identify what is truly important to you and set meaningful goals that reflect your desires. Whether it's personal, professional, or relationship-oriented goals, having a clear direction can give you a sense of accomplishment and satisfaction. Break down your goals into smaller, manageable steps and celebrate your progress along the way. By setting and pursuing meaningful goals, you create a sense of purpose and fulfillment in your life.

Practicing Self-Care

Self-care is an essential aspect of cultivating happiness and fulfillment. It involves taking deliberate actions to prioritize your physical, emotional, and mental well-being. Engage in activities that recharge and rejuvenate you, such as taking walks in nature, practicing mindfulness, or indulging in a favorite hobby. Set boundaries and learn to say no when necessary to protect your energy and avoid burnout. Remember that self-care is not selfish but rather a necessary practice to ensure your overall well-being. By prioritizing self-care, you are better equipped to show up fully in your relationships and experience greater happiness and fulfillment.

In conclusion, cultivating happiness and fulfillment as a conscious lesbian dater requires a commitment to self-reflection, self-care, and personal growth. By embracing gratitude, pursuing passions, nurturing relationships, practicing mindfulness, cultivating self-compassion, setting meaningful goals, and prioritizing self-care, you can create a life that is rich in happiness and fulfillment. Remember that your happiness is not dependent on external factors but rather an internal journey that you have the power to navigate. Embrace the process, be kind to yourself, and enjoy the journey of cultivating happiness and fulfillment in your life.

8

Chapter 8

Celebrating Love and Community

8.1 Embracing LGBTQ+ Community

In the journey of conscious lesbian dating and love, it is essential to embrace and celebrate the LGBTQ+ community. The LGBTQ+ community is a diverse and vibrant group of individuals who share a common experience of non-heterosexual or non-cisgender identities. By embracing this community, you not only show support and solidarity but also open yourself up to a world of understanding, acceptance, and love.

Understanding LGBTQ+ Terminology

To fully embrace the LGBTQ+ community, it is important to have a basic understanding of the terminology used within the community. This will help you communicate respectfully and avoid unintentionally causing harm. Here are a few key terms to familiarize yourself with:

1. Lesbian: A woman who is emotionally, romantically, and/or sexually attracted to other women.
2. Gay: A term often used to describe men who are emotionally, romantically, and/or sexually attracted to other men. It can also be used as an umbrella term for the entire LGBTQ+ community.
3. Bisexual: An individual who is emotionally, romantically, and/or sexually attracted to both men and women.
4. Transgender: A person whose gender identity differs from the sex they were assigned at birth.
5. Queer: An umbrella term used to describe individuals who do not identify as heterosexual or cisgender. It can also be used as a self-identifying term for individuals within the LGBTQ+ community.
6. Non-binary: An umbrella term for individuals who do not exclusively identify as male or female.
7. Pansexual: An individual who is emotionally, romantically, and/or sexually attracted to people regardless of their gender identity or biological sex.
8. Ally: A person who supports and advocates for the rights and well-being of the LGBTQ+ community, even if they do not personally identify as LGBTQ+.

Creating Inclusive Spaces

Embracing the LGBTQ+ community involves creating inclusive spaces where everyone feels welcome and accepted. Whether you are hosting a social gathering, attending an event, or simply engaging in conversations, here are some ways to create inclusive spaces:

1. Use inclusive language: Be mindful of the language you use and avoid assumptions about someone's gender identity or sexual orientation. Use gender-neutral terms whenever possible.
2. Educate yourself: Take the time to educate yourself about LGBTQ+ history, issues, and experiences. This will help you better understand and empathize with the community.
3. Challenge stereotypes: Challenge and confront any stereotypes or prejudices you may encounter, both within yourself and in others. Advocate for equality and challenge discriminatory behavior.
4. Be an ally: Show your support for the LGBTQ+ community by being an ally. This means actively listening, learning, and advocating for LGBTQ+ rights and equality.
5. Respect pronouns: Respect and use the correct pronouns for individuals. If you are unsure, ask politely or use gender-neutral pronouns such as they/them until you receive clarification.
6. Celebrate diversity: Embrace and celebrate the diversity within the LGBTQ+ community. Recognize that each individual's experience is unique and valid.

Getting Involved in LGBTQ+ Organizations and Events

One of the best ways to embrace the LGBTQ+ community is by getting involved in LGBTQ+ organizations and events. These spaces provide opportunities to connect with like-minded individuals, learn from their experiences, and contribute to the community. Here are some ways to get involved:

1. Attend LGBTQ+ events: Look for local LGBTQ+ events such

as pride parades, film festivals, or community gatherings. These events are not only fun but also provide a chance to meet new people and celebrate diversity.
2. Volunteer: Many LGBTQ+ organizations rely on volunteers to support their initiatives. Consider volunteering your time and skills to help create positive change within the community.
3. Join LGBTQ+ support groups: Support groups provide a safe and supportive environment for individuals to share their experiences and seek guidance. Joining a support group can help you connect with others who understand your journey.
4. Advocate for LGBTQ+ rights: Stand up for LGBTQ+ rights by participating in advocacy campaigns, signing petitions, or contacting your local representatives. Your voice can make a difference in creating a more inclusive society.
5. Support LGBTQ+ businesses: Seek out and support LGBTQ+-owned businesses in your community. By doing so, you contribute to the economic empowerment of the community.

Educating Others and Spreading Awareness

As you embrace the LGBTQ+ community, it is important to educate others and spread awareness. By sharing your knowledge and experiences, you can help create a more inclusive and accepting society. Here are some ways to educate others:

1. Engage in conversations: Be open to having conversations about LGBTQ+ issues and experiences. Share your own journey and listen to others with empathy and respect.

2. Share resources: Recommend books, articles, documentaries, or podcasts that provide insights into LGBTQ+ experiences. Sharing resources can help others expand their understanding and challenge their preconceptions.
3. Challenge misconceptions: When you encounter misconceptions or stereotypes about the LGBTQ+ community, gently challenge them with facts and personal experiences. Encourage others to question their biases and learn more.
4. Be a role model: By living authentically and embracing your own identity, you become a role model for others. Your visibility and confidence can inspire and empower those who may be struggling with their own identities.

Embracing the LGBTQ+ community is not only about acceptance but also about actively supporting and advocating for equality and inclusivity. By creating inclusive spaces, getting involved in LGBTQ+ organizations, educating others, and celebrating diversity, you contribute to a world where love and acceptance thrive. Remember, love knows no boundaries, and by embracing the LGBTQ+ community, you open yourself up to a world of beautiful connections and experiences.

8.2 Supporting and Advocating for LGBTQ+ Rights

As a conscious lesbian, it is important to not only focus on your own dating and love life but also to actively support and advocate for LGBTQ+ rights. By doing so, you contribute to creating a more inclusive and accepting society for yourself and others. This section will explore various ways you can support and advocate for LGBTQ+ rights.

Educate Yourself

One of the first steps in supporting and advocating for LGBTQ+ rights is to educate yourself about the issues faced by the community. Take the time to learn about the history of LGBTQ+ rights movements, the challenges faced by different identities within the community, and the progress that has been made. By understanding the struggles and triumphs of the LGBTQ+ community, you can better advocate for their rights.

Speak Out

Using your voice to speak out against discrimination and inequality is a powerful way to support LGBTQ+ rights. Whether it's in your personal relationships, at work, or in your community, don't be afraid to challenge homophobic or transphobic comments and behaviors. By speaking up, you can help create a safer and more inclusive environment for everyone.

Support LGBTQ+ Organizations

There are numerous organizations dedicated to advocating for LGBTQ+ rights. Consider supporting these organizations through donations, volunteering, or participating in their events and campaigns. Your support can help fund important initiatives, provide resources to those in need, and amplify the voices of the LGBTQ+ community.

Vote for LGBTQ+ Friendly Policies and Candidates

Voting is a powerful tool for change. Research candidates and their positions on LGBTQ+ rights before casting your vote. Support candidates who are committed to advancing LGBTQ+ rights and policies that promote equality and inclusivity. By voting for LGBTQ+ friendly candidates, you can help shape the future of your community and country.

Attend LGBTQ+ Events and Pride Parades

Attending LGBTQ+ events and pride parades is a great way to show your support and solidarity. These events provide an opportunity to celebrate the LGBTQ+ community, raise awareness about LGBTQ+ issues, and connect with like-minded individuals. By participating in these events, you contribute to the visibility and acceptance of the LGBTQ+ community.

Use Social Media for Advocacy

Social media platforms offer a powerful tool for advocacy. Use your online presence to share information, resources, and stories related to LGBTQ+ rights. Amplify the voices of LGBTQ+ activists and organizations by sharing their content. Engage in respectful discussions and challenge misinformation or prejudice when you come across it. By using social media for advocacy, you can reach a wide audience and contribute to changing hearts and minds.

Support LGBTQ+ Owned Businesses

Supporting LGBTQ+ owned businesses is another way to show your support for the community. Seek out and patronize businesses that are owned and operated by LGBTQ+ individuals. By doing so, you contribute to the economic empowerment of the community and help create a more inclusive business landscape.

Be an Ally

Being an ally means actively supporting and advocating for the rights of the LGBTQ+ community, even if you do not identify as LGBTQ+ yourself. Educate yourself about LGBTQ+ issues, listen to the experiences and perspectives of LGBTQ+ individuals, and use your privilege to amplify their voices. Be open to learning and growing, and be willing to challenge your own biases and assumptions. By being an ally, you can help create a more inclusive and accepting world for all.

Support LGBTQ+ Youth

LGBTQ+ youth often face unique challenges and are at a higher risk of experiencing discrimination, bullying, and mental health issues. Support LGBTQ+ youth by volunteering with organizations that provide resources and support to young people. Be a mentor or a role model, and create a safe and accepting space for LGBTQ+ youth in your community. By supporting LGBTQ+ youth, you contribute to their well-being and help shape a brighter future for the community.

Advocate for LGBTQ+ Inclusive Policies

Advocating for LGBTQ+ inclusive policies at the local, national, and international levels is crucial for advancing LGBTQ+ rights. Stay informed about proposed policies and legislation that impact the LGBTQ+ community, and reach out to your elected officials to express your support or concerns. Join or start campaigns to push for LGBTQ+ inclusive policies in areas such as healthcare, education, employment, and housing. By advocating for LGBTQ+ inclusive policies, you can help create a more equitable society for all.

Supporting and advocating for LGBTQ+ rights is an ongoing commitment. By actively engaging in these actions, you contribute to the progress and well-being of the LGBTQ+ community. Remember, every effort, no matter how small, makes a difference. Together, we can create a world where love and acceptance thrive for all.

8.3 Creating Meaningful Connections

Creating meaningful connections is an essential aspect of conscious lesbian dating and love. It involves building deep and authentic relationships with others that go beyond surface-level interactions. Meaningful connections are based on mutual understanding, respect, and shared values, and they can bring immense joy and fulfillment to your life. In this section, we will explore various ways to create meaningful connections in your dating journey and beyond.

1. Be Present and Authentic

One of the most important aspects of creating meaningful connections is being present and authentic in your interactions. When you are fully present, you are able to listen actively and engage with others in a genuine way. This means putting away distractions, such as your phone, and giving your full attention to the person you are connecting with.

Authenticity is also crucial in building meaningful connections. It involves being true to yourself and expressing your thoughts, feelings, and desires honestly. When you are authentic, you allow others to see the real you, which can foster deeper connections based on trust and understanding.

2. Practice Active Listening

Active listening is a powerful tool for creating meaningful connections. It involves fully focusing on the speaker and seeking to understand their perspective without judgment or interruption. When you practice active listening, you show respect and empathy towards the other person, which can strengthen your connection.

To practice active listening, give your undivided attention to the speaker, maintain eye contact, and provide verbal and non-verbal cues to show that you are engaged. Reflecting back what the speaker has said and asking clarifying questions can also demonstrate your commitment to understanding their thoughts and feelings.

3. Share Vulnerability

Creating meaningful connections often requires vulnerability. It involves opening up and sharing your authentic self, including your fears, insecurities, and past experiences. By sharing vulnerability, you create a safe space for others to do the same, which can deepen your connection and foster intimacy.

However, it's important to remember that vulnerability should be reciprocated and respected. It's not about oversharing or burdening others with your emotional baggage. Instead, it's about finding a balance and gradually opening up as trust is established in the relationship.

4. Engage in Meaningful Conversations

Meaningful connections are built through meaningful conversations. Engaging in deep and thought-provoking discussions can help you understand others on a deeper level and create a sense of connection. Instead of sticking to small talk, try to explore topics that are important to you and your potential partner.

Ask open-ended questions that encourage the other person to share their thoughts and feelings. Be curious and genuinely interested in their responses. By actively participating in meaningful conversations, you can create a space for intellectual and emotional connection to flourish.

5. Seek Shared Values and Goals

Creating meaningful connections is easier when you share common values and goals with the people you are connecting with. Shared values provide a foundation for understanding and compatibility, while shared goals can create a sense of purpose and direction in the relationship.

Take the time to explore your own values and goals, and be open to discovering those of others. When you find someone who aligns with your core values and shares similar aspirations, it can strengthen your connection and create a solid basis for a meaningful relationship.

6. Foster Mutual Growth and Support

Meaningful connections thrive when there is mutual growth and support. Encourage and support the personal and professional development of the people you are connecting with. Celebrate their achievements and provide a listening ear during challenging times.

Similarly, seek growth and support from others. Surround yourself with individuals who inspire and uplift you. By fostering mutual growth and support, you create a network of meaningful connections that can contribute to your overall happiness and fulfillment.

7. Embrace Diversity and Inclusion

Creating meaningful connections involves embracing diversity and inclusion. Recognize and appreciate the unique perspectives and experiences that others bring to the table. Be open to learning from different backgrounds and cultures, and challenge any biases or prejudices you may hold.

By embracing diversity and inclusion, you create an environment where everyone feels valued and respected. This can lead to deeper connections and a broader understanding of the world around you.

8. Practice Gratitude and Appreciation

Expressing gratitude and appreciation is a powerful way to create meaningful connections. Take the time to acknowledge and thank the people who have positively impacted your life. Show appreciation for their presence, support, and contributions.

By practicing gratitude and appreciation, you not only strengthen your existing connections but also attract more meaningful relationships into your life. It cultivates a positive and nurturing environment where love and connection can flourish.

Creating meaningful connections is an ongoing process that requires effort and intentionality. By being present, authentic, and open to vulnerability, you can build deep and fulfilling relationships with others. Remember to engage in meaningful conversations, seek shared values and goals, and foster mutual growth and support. Embrace diversity and practice gratitude and appreciation to create a network of meaningful connections that enrich your life.

8.4 Celebrating Love and Relationships

Love is a beautiful and powerful force that deserves to be celebrated. As a conscious lesbian, it is important to honor and cherish the love and relationships in your life. Celebrating love not only brings joy and happiness but also strengthens the bond between you and your partner. In this section, we will explore different ways to celebrate love and relationships as a conscious lesbian.

1. Expressing Gratitude

One of the simplest yet most powerful ways to celebrate love is by expressing gratitude. Take a moment each day to reflect on the love and support you receive from your partner. Acknowledge the little things they do that make your life better and let them know how much you appreciate them. Whether it's a heartfelt thank you, a love note, or a small gesture of kindness, expressing gratitude can deepen your connection and create a positive atmosphere in your relationship.

2. Quality Time

Spending quality time together is essential for nurturing and celebrating your love. Set aside dedicated time to be fully present with your partner, free from distractions. Engage in activities that you both enjoy, such as going for walks, cooking together, or having a movie night. Use this time to connect on a deeper level, share your thoughts and feelings, and create lasting memories. Quality time allows you to strengthen your bond and celebrate the unique connection you share.

3. Celebrating Milestones

Milestones in a relationship are worth celebrating. Whether it's your anniversary, a special date, or a significant achievement, take the time to acknowledge and celebrate these milestones together. Plan a romantic dinner, surprise your partner with a thoughtful gift, or create a scrapbook of your memories. Celebrating milestones not only shows your partner that you value and cherish your relationship, but it also allows you to reflect on how far you've come together.

4. Creating Rituals

Rituals can be a beautiful way to celebrate love and relationships. They provide a sense of continuity and create a shared experience between you and your partner. Consider creating rituals that hold special meaning for both of you, such as a weekly date night, a monthly adventure, or an annual getaway. These rituals can become cherished traditions that strengthen your bond and give you something to look forward to as a couple.

5. Supporting Each Other's Dreams

Celebrating love also means supporting each other's dreams and aspirations. Take the time to understand your partner's goals and dreams, and actively support them in pursuing them. Whether it's starting a new business, going back to school, or exploring a new hobby, be their biggest cheerleader. Celebrate their achievements, no matter how big or small, and be there to provide encouragement and support along the way. By celebrating each other's dreams, you create a foundation of love and support that can withstand any challenge.

6. Acts of Kindness

Small acts of kindness can go a long way in celebrating love and relationships. Surprise your partner with breakfast in bed, leave them a sweet note, or do something thoughtful that shows you care. These acts of kindness not only make your partner feel loved and appreciated but also create a positive and loving atmosphere in your relationship. Celebrate love by consistently showing up for each other and making each other's lives a little brighter.

7. Celebrating Individuality

In a conscious lesbian relationship, it is important to celebrate and honor each other's individuality. Embrace and celebrate the unique qualities and strengths that you and your partner bring to the relationship. Encourage each other to pursue personal growth and self-discovery. Celebrate the milestones and achievements in each other's lives, whether they are related to your relationship or not. By celebrating each other's individuality, you create a space where both partners can thrive and grow together.

8. Sharing Love with the Community

Celebrating love and relationships extends beyond your partnership. As a conscious lesbian, you can celebrate love by sharing your experiences and wisdom with the LGBTQ+ community. Attend pride events, participate in LGBTQ+ organizations, and engage in conversations that promote love and acceptance. By sharing your love and experiences, you contribute to a more inclusive and supportive community for all.

Conclusion

Love is a precious gift that deserves to be celebrated. As a conscious lesbian, you have the power to create a loving and fulfilling relationship. By expressing gratitude, spending quality time, celebrating milestones, creating rituals, supporting each other's dreams, performing acts of kindness, celebrating individuality, and sharing love with the community, you can celebrate love and relationships in a meaningful and authentic way. Remember, love is a journey, and every step along the way is worth celebrating.

Afterword

Congratulations on completing this transformative journey through the pages of this book. The path to discovering your authentic self in the world of lesbian dating and love is indeed a remarkable, challenging, and deeply fulfilling endeavor. As you reach the end of this book, it is our hope that you have gained not only knowledge but also the courage and wisdom to embark on the ongoing process of self-discovery, self-acceptance, and self-love.

Understanding and embracing your authentic self is not a destination; it's a lifelong journey. It's a voyage that will be filled with highs and lows, self-discovery, and the continuous pursuit of personal growth. The complexities of our identities, the intricacies of our desires, and the ever-evolving landscape of our emotions make this journey a truly remarkable one.

Lesbian dating and love have their unique challenges, but the lessons learned in these chapters can apply to anyone, regardless of their sexual orientation. The fundamental truth, which has been a recurring theme throughout this book, is that to find love, you must first be the love that you seek.

At times, the dating world can feel daunting, as if it demands you to be someone you're not. It may seem like you need to fit into a certain mold, conform to societal expectations, or bend yourself to meet the preferences of others. But remember, authenticity is your greatest asset. The more you embrace your true self, the more magnetic and attractive you become to the right people who are meant to be a part of your life.

Your journey to authenticity and self-love involves letting go of past hurts, facing your insecurities, and embracing your uniqueness. It is a journey that requires you to be patient with yourself, forgiving of your past mistakes, and open to the lessons they have to offer.

www.ingramcontent.com/pod-product-compliance
Ingram Content Group UK Ltd.
Pitfield, Milton Keynes, MK11 3LW, UK
UKHW021649190726
13853UKWH00001B/143